When
Your Child
Is Deaf

D1003131

WHEN YOUR CHILD IS DEAF
A Guide for Parents

David M. Luterman, D.Ed.
with
Antonia Brancia Maxon, Ph.D.

YORK PRESS Baltimore

This book was manufactured in the United States of America. Typography by Type Shoppe II Productions, Ltd., Chestertown, Maryland.
Printing and binding by McNaughton & Gunn
Cover design by Joseph Dieter, Jr.

Library of Congress Cataloging-in-Publication Data

Luterman, David.
    When your child is deaf : a guide for parents / David M. Luterman with Antonia Brancia Maxon.--2nd ed.
        p. cm.
    Includes bibliographical references.
    ISBN 0-912752-66-1
        1. Parents of deaf children. 2. Child rearing. 3. Deaf children--Family relationships. 4. Deaf children--United States. I. Maxon, Antonia. II. Title.
    HQ759.913 .L87 2002
    649'.1512--dc21

                                                      2002016711

CONTENTS

Preface

Thirty-seven years ago my fifteen-month-old son was diagnosed as being profoundly deaf as a result of having had meningitis at nine months of age. We are graduates of the Thayer Lindsley Parent-Centered Nursery at Emerson College. I'd like to share with you some hindsights and insights thirty-seven years after completing that program.

I remember my own alternating feelings of pain and numbness, the disbelief of hearing that my son was deaf. So many questions began to flood my mind. Where will we turn? We knew nothing about deafness. Can he wear a hearing aid? How will he learn? Where will he go to school? Should he learn sign language or be brought up orally? How will we tell the other members of our family, especially our other kids? Where do we begin? We had already come through the trauma of almost losing him with meningitis; now we were faced with this. I had the feeling I needed to be brave, to have a stiff upper lip. What I wanted even more was to cry, to hold my child in my arms, to protect him from a world that would probably be cruel. I needed to grieve that my child wasn't "whole," that he would never hear the sound of my voice or music or leaves rustling or the ocean or birds singing. Self-pity and protection were hard enemies to fight. I felt overwhelmed, alone. We knew no one who was deaf, no adults, let alone a child.

Looking back, I realize we made an extremely important decision early on. Our choices were as follows: we would stay in self-pity and overprotection, stay in our grieving and fears, or we would seize the opportunity to see our child's deafness, believe it or not, as an asset, an opportunity to enrich his life and ours beyond measure. We would have to deal with our feelings, meet our prejudices, have a positive attitude, and grow strong. It was a tall order but we decided to follow the latter, as best we knew how. I say as best we knew how because each thing we did, each weighty decision we calculated carefully, agonizingly. What would be best? We literally did the best we knew how to do, given the educational knowledge and the emotional stability we had at that time. Then we tried to move forward without guilt. On looking back, I'm happy to say our basic decisions were good. My only educational regret is that we did not take him out of the public school system a year or so earlier and put him in a school for the deaf to catch up academically.

Being accepted into the Thayer Lindsley Nursery was the first major stepping stone after his diagnosis. What a relief it was to be accepted, to have a place to begin. It's important to risk that first beginning, to get started in a positive direction. It also marks the end of any denial that your child needs special help. In the program we had other parents to talk to, my son had a place to begin to learn, to be with other kids who couldn't hear and with a hearing child as well; I did not feel so alone. It was as if someone threw us a life line; that person was David Luterman. David expresses the insecurity he felt when he started the program, but to me, he and his wife, Cari, who taught the nursery, were refreshing and honest in their approach, giving of their knowledge, willing to grow along with us, giving me a shove in the right direction when I was discouraged or when the "poor me's" snuck in.

Since a child's attention span is so short, we were taught how to teach our child and had the opportunity to plan lessons and teach one of the other children. We taught them that different things made different sounds by feeling for the vibration; we constantly talked to them so they would learn to lip read. We learned and played and laughed and cried. In those rooms I felt supported and loved and cared about. I could get a hug and give a hug and comfort myself with a piece of Jean's, now famous to us, chocolate swirl cheesecake. It was a place where the fathers could meet to deal with their own pain and to learn and grow, and where we could meet as couples. The couples' meetings at that time made our marriage stronger, our commitment to our son and our other children more bonded.

So much of what I needed to give my children had nothing to do with our son's deafness. I now see more clearly that to overprotect is to give the message of incapability. To build self-esteem, I've learned, is the single most precious gift we can give to our children. Through this, they not only are loved but learn to love. I know also that the ability to do that comes from who I am as a person and how well I am loved and learned to love and grow. Again, all along the way, I did the very best I knew how to do at that point in time. What's really great is to realize that despite my shortcomings, my son is now in a hearing university that has a program for the deaf within the school. Last January, he traveled to Europe by himself; even he was surprised at his strength and resilience. He makes his own plane reservations using his TDD, drives a car, shares an apartment with a friend, and seems equally comfortable with his deaf friends as with his hearing friends. This certainly is to his credit and to mine, to some degree, despite my love, overprotection, personal insecurities, gifts, benign neglect, etc. The issues that he struggles with today are issues not related to his deafness.

What a gift he is to me. His deafness in so many ways has become an asset to me. How else would I have learned about the issues of deafness at all ages? I've met so many great people, other hearing-impaired individuals, parents, and professionals. I had to meet my own discomforts and prejudices about hearing aids, sign language, and deaf speech as strangers turned to stare. Yes, I still overprotect sometimes, and I still feel discomfort when I'm with young people using sign language. This discomfort comes from having raised my son orally; I never really learned to sign, so I now have to acknowledge my feelings of being left out of a conversation—a good reminder to me of what a hearing-impaired person puts up with every day.

The program also recognized the extra time and energy and patience it took for us to deal with our deaf child. We scheduled special trips to include our other children and also made them part of the daily lessons at home. They did some teaching, too. I tried to give my other children special time; I was not always successful at this. Despite my shortcomings, my two boys have a closer relationship today than ever before. My son moved to California to go to college but also to be close to his sister whom he adores. They are not as close as they used to be, but again not because of issues related to his deafness.

As you read this today, your distinct advantage over mine will be the thirty-seven years of foundation that open opportunities unavailable to us. Physicians are more knowledgeable about deafness, as are local school systems. Medical technology has advanced (e.g., cochlear implants), hearing aids have been improved, there are books like this to read and refined established programs and new programs to consider.

My faith has been a foundation for stability and hope. It has grown profoundly over the past years. It is important to me to know there is a power greater than myself to help me deal with whatever comes in my life's journey.

Yes, your life, like mine, will be a mix of sorrows and joys, weighty decisions and fun, carefree times. I have learned that it is in the midst of my pain and struggle that I gain the most growth.

Our sorrows and our joys are inseparable. Our tears arise from the same place as our laughter; perhaps that's why great laughter is often accompanied by tears. The greater the joy we feel, the greater is the potential for our sorrow. I want always to risk being vulnerable, to love and invest myself in a relationship, whether it is with my deaf child or another family member or a friend. I accept the difficult times so much more easily and look for the blessings.

May you be filled with hope, for there is much. I wish you patience, love, the gift of careful decisions, quiet times to savor your life in its goodness, valleys to explore, still waters to restore you, mountains to climb, gentleness, strength, and forgiveness.

May your child be a blessing to you, but even more importantly, may you be a blessing to your child.

Carol Ann Youngdahl

Introduction

I began my professional life forty years ago as a clinical audiologist. I am still not sure what prompted me to select this field. I can recall, at a time when I was casting about to find a profession, an elderly teacher of public speaking saying that if he had it to do over again, he would become a speech pathologist or an audiologist. I think I took him up on his dream and I have no regrets for having done so.

I began working at Emerson College both as an academician, teaching undergraduate and graduate courses in audiology, and as a clinician in the Speech and Hearing Center associated with the college program. After a few years, I began to realize that audiology was not for me. You know you are in trouble in your profession when you begin to hope that clients won't show up. For me a good day was one with several cancellations. I was happy with the teaching and living in the New England area, so I looked for a way to relate to the field other than as a clinical audiologist. It occurred to me quite early in my career that parents of deaf children were not being treated well—least of all by me. I followed the prescribed procedure, which I had learned in my training program, for testing the hearing of young children: this involved first taking a detailed case history and then trying to separate the child from the parent. As graduate students, we were always advised to do this because we were told the parents might interfere with the test procedures and might bias the results. In actuality, I think it was because we were afraid of parents; afraid that they might detect our mistakes and our often rather fumbling attempts to obtain a reliable audiogram on a young child. When I did test a child successfully and found a hearing loss present, I would then go into the waiting room and in my best Marcus Welby manner tell the anxious parents that their child had a hearing loss. At this point, I usually floundered.

I knew that the parents were very upset and needed to cry, but I did not have any experience in handling grief. In addition to being anxious about delivering the bad news, I think I knew intuitively that people often kill the messenger when they don't like the message. I was fearful of the parents' possible angry reaction. I also think I felt vaguely guilty that I had caused pain.

Counseling, as defined by my supervisor, was synonymous with giving information. By keeping the counseling centered on information, I did not have to deal with those messy feeling that I had no experience in handling. As a matter of fact, I can remember vague supervisory injunctions not to get into feelings; if feelings did emerge, I was to refer the parent to the clinic psychologist for "counseling."

After a few years of clinical work, I began to develop "tapes." These were set speeches that I would give to parents which served to forestall the tears as they forced the parents to take a cognitive tack. There were "tapes" about the audiogram, hearing aids, and educational options. Parents would often listen with glazed-over eyes, nodding their heads and wishing they could go somewhere and cry. I would drone on, finish my "tape," and then refer them to an educational program where I assumed, erroneously, their needs would be met. In all sincerity, I thought I was doing a good job.

After a few years, when parents would return for a reevaluation of their child's hearing, I began to discover that I hadn't been very effective. Parents were asking me questions about material that I thought I had covered so well; speeches that I had been giving parents literally went in one ear and out the other. I discovered that when I had poured out all that information, their feelings had been so high and dominant that they hadn't been able to grasp anything I had said. Not only was I wasting my time, but I also was contributing to their fear and panic.

Parents normally feel overwhelmed when told they have a hearing-impaired child, and when they are burdened with gratuitous information that they can't absorb, it only increases their feelings of inadequacy. I discovered also that the educational programs to which I referred the parents did just as poor a job educating and involving the parents as I did. Teachers of the deaf, I found, were just as insecure dealing with parents as I was as a clinical audiologist. Each of us had little training in this area. Because of our professional insecurity, parents in school programs were talked at and lectured at, but rarely *listened to*. They were invariably invited to visit the school under very controlled situations and were encouraged to raise funds for the school. Parents rarely were treated as equals in the awesome task of educating their hearing-impaired child. (A great deal of lip-service was given to parent-teacher equality, but in practice, the teacher's skills and knowledge were valued more than anything parents had to offer.)

So, there I was in 1965, dismayed by my own lack of skill in dealing with parents and so disenchanted with the field of clinical audiology that I decided to start a family-centered nursery program for hearing-impaired children. I now look back on how little I

knew at the time and marvel at my temerity in starting a program to educate families. At times, though, I
think it is necessary simply to leap into the professional world; what I lacked in information and skills, I
made up for in commitment and enthusiasm. Fortunately I was blessed with marvelous parents to work
with, especially in the first few years of the program.
And they treated me gently, forgiving my mistakes and
teaching me a great deal. Many of them have remained
my friends through the years.

When I started the program, I thought I would do
it for a year or two and then go on to something else. I
wasn't sure what the "something else" was but I thought
the nursery was a bridge to it. Well, thirty-five years later,
I am still on the "bridge," and I have found for myself an
endlessly fascinating life work. I cannot conceive of doing
anything other than what I am now doing and I marvel
that I am paid for it. I have never been bored by working
intimately with parents of newly diagnosed hearing-
impaired children.

The program, as designed, was a transition program
for parents as they moved from the diagnosis of their
child's loss into the educational establishment. Parents
were invited to enroll in our nursery program for an academic year before moving on to a school for the deaf. They
were required to come with their child two mornings a
week (later increased to three). We insisted that the parents must attend: "dropping off" the child was not acceptable. We defined "parent" loosely to be any primary
caregiver, and over the years we have had nannies, grandparents, and aunts bring children; occasionally families
have been able to work it out so that father and mother
could alternate attendance, although most of the time it
has been the mothers who have come. The nursery room
is equipped with a large one-way vision mirror; adjacent to
the nursery are small therapy rooms also equipped with

one-way vision mirrors and observation booths. A typical nursery group consists of eight hearing-impaired children between the ages of 18 months and 3 years, and one or two normally hearing children.

At the beginning of the program, parents were required only to observe as the nursery teacher and graduate students (Speech/Language Pathology majors) worked with children within the group setting. During the morning, each child had an individual therapy session with a speech/language pathologist; the session aimed at improving the specific child's language and speech skills. Parents were required to watch these sessions as well. As the program progressed, parents began to work in the nursery alongside the staff and also to conduct individual therapy sessions while the therapist observed. Toward the end of the year, when visitors to the nursery would wonder who were parents and who were teachers, I knew we had a successful group.

One morning a week parents were required to attend a group session, with me as the facilitator. I can remember vividly the very first session of the nursery group when I sat at the head of the table, looked at the anxious, grief stricken faces of the parents, and wondered what in the world I was doing there. I knew that my few "tapes," which had served me well in the short-term contact that is typical between audiologist and parent, would not serve for long-term commitment of a support group. An academic year was composed of two 15-week semesters, and each group session was 90 minutes long. I couldn't fake it for that length of time, so I had all the parents introduce themselves and relate how they had gotten into the program. When everyone had finished, I told the parents that I didn't know what was supposed to happen in the group, but I hoped that they would become comfortable there. (Actually, I was hoping I would be comfortable there.) A long silence followed as everybody looked around at everybody else; the actual length of the silence was probably only 30 seconds, but it felt like hours. Then the parents began to talk to each other; their stories had triggered similar memories in the others. The talk soon became a torrent—I realized that first day, listening to the parents, how lonely they were and that all I needed to do was to give them each other in a safe environment and they would do all the work.

I found that the support group became the one place where parents felt they could be understood, where their experiences could be shared. I have found no greater gift professionals can give to parents than the gift of each other. To do this, professionals must be willing to put aside their "tapes" and to *listen*. The parents will teach them much. I have found that parents learn more when I listen than when I talk.

Despite my appalling ignorance at the inception of the program, I can see, in retrospect, that I intuitively did many things right. I knew that I had to keep the focus on parents and not let the professionals and myself be "seduced" by the children. I continually had to remind everyone that if we took good care of the parents, the children would turn out well. In thirty-seven years of working in the program I have seen nothing to contradict that statement; if anything, it has been reinforced repeatedly by my clinical experience.

The other premise of the program was that we take care of the human needs before the "special" needs. I had met too many "successful" deaf adults who had good oral skills but were unhappy human beings with limited capacity for joy and satisfactory interpersonal relations; I counted them as failures. I did not want to repeat the mistakes of the past, and I wanted to be sure that we treated the children as children first. I hired a nursery teacher who was not a teacher of the deaf. Her task was to keep the staff focused on the developmental issues and to keep reminding us that these were children who happened to have a hearing loss. To that end, we also included a hearing child in the nursery (the first one was my third-born child), not to stimulate the language of deaf children—since two-year-olds do not talk with one another very much— but to remind staff and parents alike what the developmental issues are with a two-year-old. For example, there is no deafer creature on the face of this earth than a two-year-old, with or without a hearing deficit. Parents continually confuse developmental issues with deafness issues. In my experience, parents invariably give their child too much credit for being deaf but do not discipline the child appropriately, or have too low expectations for the child's behavior. I think the biggest obstacle for deaf children is the low expectations that parents and teachers have.

In our program, we have never altered the basic notions of always keeping parents as our first responsibility and staying continually focused on the human needs—it has paid big dividends.

This book reflects what parents have taught me over the past thirty-seven years of participation in support groups. I feel privileged to have been permitted to be a part of the process by which parents learn to cope with the responsibilities of raising a deaf child. Parents need help raising their deaf child and in making their way through the morass of issues in education of the deaf and in audiological practice. Most educational programs for parents seem to be confounded by professional biases and are rarely truly educational, focussing instead on brain-washing parents into a particular educational philosophy. There are several books that have been written for parents that I have not found satisfactory either, because they present a biased or incomplete view of the field. In fact, the origins of this book stem from my being asked by a scholarly journal to review a book for parents. I found the book awful—I knew I could do a much better job.

The twenty-fifth anniversary of the nursery program prompted me to do two things: one, to survey all known graduates of our program, and two, to begin the first edition of this book. I hope the second edition, like the first, becomes a useful reference for parents of newly diagnosed hearing-impaired children. I intend to provide information for parents about the emotional process of coming to grips with a hearing impairment in their child; and also about the impact of hearing loss on the parenting processes and on the extended family. Information is also provided on current audiological practice, amplifying systems, and educational philosophy. The chapters on amplifying systems and audiological process are written by my friend Toni Maxon, who, in addition to remaining in clinical audiological practice, was also a professor training audiologists at the University of Connecticut. The last chapter, "Parent to Parent," is my selection from written advice gleaned from the survey of graduates of our program. As such, it represents hundreds of years of accumulated parental wisdom.

There is always a certain amount of arrogance in writing any book. But I now think, after working intimately with parents of hearing-impaired children for the past thirty-seven years, that I have a sufficient grasp of the awesome task of raising a hearing-impaired child; you, the reader, must judge how successful I've been.

Acknowledgments

Authorship of a book is always deceptive. Even though there is one author's name, or two, there are really many people who contribute to the final product. My wife, Cari, was a tough editor and a good person to bounce ideas off; and Helen Ross is an even tougher editor. I am deeply indebted to Polly Meltzer and Julie Rubin Goldberg who read the manuscript and offered many helpful suggestions. They were the nursery school teacher and the supervising therapist of the Emerson program. It was their gritty day-to-day work that makes the program what it is; they also made me look good. My friends Sue Colten, Margaret Lahey, and Jack Roush read and commented on chapters of the manuscript. Toni Maxon contributed two very readable chapters about difficult technical material that I could not do.

I am forever grateful to the parents who, through the years, have taught me so much. Each parent group leaves me richer and I would have dedicated this book to them, except that my children love to see their names in print. I am also indebted to the Massachusetts Parents' Association for the Deaf. I commandeered, in part, the title of its marvelous directory of services for this book's title. It is an organization that I have long admired.

For my children, Alison, Daniel, Emily, and James, and their spouses, Vicky, Sairey, and David, and for the miracles that are Joshua, Brandon, Noah, Theo, Jarid, and Eli, my grandsons. You taught me so much—so as to make this book possible.

CHAPTER I

The Feelings of Deafness

If you are the typical hearing parents of a deaf child,[1] this might be the scenario: One of you, usually the mother, begins to suspect that there is something wrong with your child. The first fear that enters your mind is that the child might be retarded. After a while, you begin to suspect hearing loss is the problem. At this point, usually when the child is about six months of age, you confide your fears to your husband. He invariably responds by denying the whole thing and reassures you that you are just being a nervous mother. Then, when you are away, he surreptitiously begins to test the baby's hearing, just as you do when he is not home. A husband's reassurance seldom lasts long and only serves to force the wife to keep her anxiety to herself.

When an inexperienced person, especially an already biased one, tries to test the hearing of an infant, the results are usually inconclusive. Even though the child may have a significant hearing loss, a stimulus that is loud enough can exceed the child's threshold and you can get a legitimate response. If you are not careful, you may also get a great many false-positive responses: when you bang two pots together to make a sound or when you clap your hands loudly, you may also cast a shadow on the wall, create a pressure wave, or produce the stimulus so that the child can sense movement with his or her peripheral vision. (Deaf children learn early to be very sensitive to visual and tactile stimuli to compensate for their reduced hearing ability.)

During this period (the child is now six months to a year old), you are on an emotional roller coaster—happy when you get a response or a pseudoresponse and dejected when you fail to get any response at all.

Finally, you admit to each other that there may be something wrong with your child's hearing, and you seek the help of a professional. Usually this is the family pediatrician. I wish I could, in this scenario, tell you that the pediatrician is "with it" and quickly refers you to an audiological/otological facility. Unfortunately, in many instances, the pediatrician responds as did the father/husband and tries to reassure the mother that everything is okay or gives inadequate and inappropriate hearing tests with the same equivocal results that the parents obtained. In a survey of parents of deaf children several years ago we asked parents at what age they first suspected a hearing loss (6 months), and at what age the diagnosis was confirmed (17 months). That eleven month gap between seeking help and receiving confirmation was, in many cases, due to the pediatrician's reluctance to refer. We are finding now, in the greater Boston area at any rate, that the ages of diagnostic confirmation are lowering and we are seeing more and more infants under a year old in our clinic. There also seem to be fewer pediatric "horror stories" told by the parents. I think there is now a greater sensitivity to the concerns of parents by the medical community, helped in no small measure by the parents' willingness to confront pediatricians with their mistakes.

When you and your husband finally make your way to the otological/audiological facility and have the diagnosis confirmed, your initial reaction very often is one of relief on two counts: first, finally somebody believes you and, thus, is validating your perception; and second, your child is not retarded; at this point you do not, as most people do not, recognize the dimension of deafness. During the interim between the pediatric referral and the audiological confirmation you may have been consoling yourself with the notion that the doctors can "fix it." "Look," think you, "they put men on the moon, they transplant hearts, surely they can fix my baby's hearing." It's when you are told unequivocally that the hearing loss is not curable and that your child will have to wear hearing aids for the rest of his or her life that the emotional impact occurs.

This scenario of gradual parental awareness and parent-initiated diagnosis, is rapidly becoming extinct, being replaced by universal screening of newborns. In this instance, unsuspecting parents, one or two days post-partum, are informed by hospital personnel that their child might have a hearing loss. This is now an institution-initiated model of diagnosis and presents parents with a somewhat different picture. Parents who have experienced this institution-initiated model have told me that the wait between the hospital screening and the audiological appointment where the loss was confirmed was interminable. Here too the parents constantly test the child to see if the loss is real at a time when they should be adjusting to having a newborn baby. Many parents who experienced newborn screening have told me that they were grateful that they found out so early so that they could initiate habilitation, but they all mourn the fact that they never had a chance to truly enjoy the baby. Regardless of when a parent finds that their child is hearing impaired, the emotional impact is the same. (More information on newborn screening can be found in Chapter 5.) At first you feel almost numb: this is the shock stage, a divorcement of self from action. For a long while you will feel as though you are walking through someone's else's nightmare, with everything feeling unreal.

One mother told how each morning she would wake up sure her child could hear, then run into her room and try to wake the child by calling her. When the child couldn't respond, the mother's devastation would begin again. It was as if she woke up each day dreaming.

Probably the predominant feeling that emerges next is the feeling of being overwhelmed—of being inadequate to the task of raising a deaf child. All parents are scared. Merely being a parent is such an awesome responsibility that any parent who is the least bit introspective about the process recognizes the fundamental fears that all parents possess. The thought of raising this child to responsible adulthood is overwhelming and all parents "run scared." Generally, we lose sight of this fear in the day-to-day raising of our children. It is only in those extraordinary times when the child gets into trouble (and children have an incredible knack for doing this) that we recognize anew our fundamental fears. This is exactly what happens when you are told that your child is deaf, the latent fear emerges and overwhelms you, because not only is your child now special—you will have to be also; you wonder if you are up to the task. This recognition of your "Specialness" and the awesome sense of responsibility it generates leaves you feeling scared.

The anxiety and the feelings of inadequacy tend to play themselves out in trying to find a savior, someone who will know the right answer and resolve much of the confusion you are feeling. There is always peril in this because there are many would-be saviors in the deafness field, most of whom are in conflict with each other, and instead of having your confusion and fear resolved, it is only intensified. It becomes hard for you to know whom to trust, despite the fact that there are many caring and competent professionals in the field. The overwhelming anxiety displays itself often as a feeling of being out-of-control. At this point, your life as you knew it has been taken from you, and in a desperate attempt to get it back you search frantically for answers, especially any answer that will promise you a normal life and a child who will be able to do everything you had dreamed he or she would do. This loss of control leaves you vulnerable to the claims of any professional or pseudoprofessional who purports to be able to cure the deafness or to minimize the loss. Frequently you are running constantly seeking a cure, aided and abetted by concerned friends and relatives who have stories to tell or articles for you to read, all of which promise a miracle cure or a miracle child. At this point you are receiving so much conflicting information so quickly that you are very scared and very, very confused.

One of the things that happens when you have a deaf child is that you lose your anonymity. You stand out in a crowd. Many people, perfect strangers, wishing to help, will be willing to tell you what to do. In addition, you are having to grapple with a totally unfamiliar vocabulary. Terms such as *audiologists*, *decibel*, and *audiogram* are tossed at you casually by the professionals and you can never remember which is which. In my experience, the confusion comes about not because you have too little information but too much, too soon, and not enough time to sort it all out.

Anger is another powerful feeling that emerges from several sources. There is anger because of a violation of an expectation; it reveals itself as the "why me?" response that all parents feel, the feeling that you are being picked on and singled out—a feeling that it is all so unfair. There is also anger because of the loss of control in your life; you have suddenly lost degrees of freedom. Probably one of the angriest men I've known was a father of a seven-year-old deaf child who said:

> "I have been working all my life for a promotion in my business. I have finally gotten it and I was just made regional sales manager. If I accept the job we will have to move to a small town that has no services for deaf children. This means my child will have to go to a residential school for the deaf and I can't tolerate that—what can I do? If I take the promotion, I'll mess up my child and if I stay here, I'll mess myself up. . . ."

We all like to think we have an unlimited scope of action and can do things that are in our family's best interests. Having a deaf child is limiting and causes feelings of anger and frustration.

A third source of anger is the feeling of impotence that plays itself out as rage. All parents are pledged to make things better for their children when they are hurting. When, despite our best efforts, our children still are hurting, we feel rage—the kind of feeling that makes you want to kick the cat, put your fist through a door, or punch someone out. Most families do not have a good mechanism for handling anger. More often than not it gets displaced onto someone or something else; often this someone else is the professional who diagnosed the deafness (or didn't, as the case may be).

Domestically, little things that you would have passed over ordinarily now get blown up into huge fights; ring around the collar becomes intolerable, and your spouse's lateness for dinner without calling becomes a call to arms. The anger that is not displaced is often turned inward and suppressed; when that happens you get depressed. The depression takes the form of generalized feeling of loss and pain.There is very often not awareness of feeling, just an immense sadness and lack of energy. It takes enormous amounts of psychic energy to contain the anger, which leaves you with little energy left to deal with the rest of your life. The anger that you feel is really at the child. You think, as you look at him or her, "Why did you have to be deaf?" The anger is irrational, but normal. More accurately the anger is at the deafness that you ardently wish would go away. It is not uncommon for parents to have dreams or fantasies that their child has died. In effect, the anticipated child has died. The crushing loss, in deafness, is of the expectation that you would lead a "normal" life, and that you would have a normal-hearing child. The birth of a hearing impaired child is the loss of a dream and it is a very significant loss. As with any feelings, they need to be acknowledged; feelings just are, they are neither right nor wrong. We never should pay a price for our feelings. Behavior can be judged as to whether or not it is self-enhancing or destructive; a feeling just needs to be acknowledged and accepted.

Having a deaf child also means experiencing a profound psychological loneliness because you are cut off from all your traditional avenues of support. For example, when you seek support from your parents, and instead find that they are also grieving, you feel unsupported. In fact, they are looking to you for support and information. (This can lead to a lot of resentment.) You also find that expressing your pain is hurting them and so you keep it to yourself. When you go to your friends, you find that they really don't understand. They often try to make you feel better by telling you that it could be so much worse (for you, at this time, it couldn't be); you find yourself very angry that they have normally hearing children and you become very, very impatient with their child-rearing problems, which seem so trivial to you. Very often you find little emotional support from your husband at this time. He is struggling with his own pain and usually deals with it by cutting himself off from the rest of the family. The husband often gets heavily invested in denial, not only of his own feelings but of his wife's feelings. At this time, husbands often find a lot to do at work and limit their time at home. Emotionally, they are trying to reassure their wives that everything will turn out well, while privately they are grieving deeply. This leaves the wife/mother feeling very lonely. It is in the support group, where the mothers (and later the fathers) can meet and share their feelings, that the loneliness of deafness can be released.

Almost all mothers feel guilt. Guilt seems to be a universal emotion for women in our culture at this time. They seem to pick up guilt as a magnet picks up iron filings. In one group, a mother once said, "I even feel guilty when it rains." (My response to that was, "You must feel very powerful.") There is always a power statement in guilt, and I think the adoption of guilt is the psychological result of feeling powerless. I think guilt will be given up when women feel competent and confident in their own abilities. For you, the mother, it is easy to feel that you did something wrong during the pregnancy to cause the deafness. It is hard to carry a fetus for nine months without having something happen that, in retrospect, might appear to you to have caused the deafness. Ordinarily, you don't reveal this to anyone, but thus is born the guilty secret. Some of the guilty secrets that mothers have shared with me:

> "I didn't take good care of myself the first two months of my pregnancy; I smoked and drank."

> "I took a lot of sauna baths while I was pregnant."
> "I ran to catch a bus and that precipitated labor and that is why he was born premature with a hearing loss."

> "I wore high heels to the cocktail party and that is why I fell down stairs. I am sure the fall caused the deafness."

If you can't find something in your pregnancy to blame, perhaps you search your premarital life to find out why God is punishing you. It's not hard to find some "sin" you committed that will account for the guilt you feel.

Father guilt rarely is focused on causes of deafness, although parents who suspect a genetic cause of the deafness often minutely examine each other's family trees; occasionally a father will feel some guilt that he contributed a defective gene. This is known as "the blame game" and parents frequently indulge in this shortly after the diagnosis. This is usually a very destructive game with no winners, only losers. No hearing parent wants to have a deaf child. More often than not, however, even when there is a definite genetic cause for the deafness, the wife/mother will take full responsibility anyway; it is as though mothers feel they contribute one hundred percent of the genes themselves, especially if they are "bad" genes.

Father guilt usually centers around the failure to defend the family. The father's role in the family is to stand at the gates and slay any dragons that might be attacking; when someone is hurting, he has failed.

This is why fathers/husbands can seldom tolerate expressions of pain from family members. They often experience the pain of others as a failure on their part —so they try distracting the family member when all that is needed is for them to listen and acknowledge the pain. Very few husbands, especially when they are in pain themselves, can do this. Husbands must be released from their protector roles before they can grieve and acknowledge their own pain.

Both parents also wonder whether they have done enough—from the father's perspective: Have I done enough to find a cure?; from the mother's perspective: Am I doing enough to ameliorate the deafness?

Guilt often manifests itself in the super-dedicated parent—one who says, "I let something bad happen to you once. Now, I'm going to make it up to you, kid." This guilt drives you to find one more doctor, to attend one more lecture, to give the extra lesson, usually at great cost to you and the rest of your family members. The price you pay for being super-dedicated usually shows up much later with a disfunctional family. Your marriage can suffer because you have put so much of your energy into the parenting that there is little left for the marriage. Siblings may become at risk because they are often enlisted as quasi-therapists; they suffer from the turmoil in the family and seldom get the attention they need from exhausted parents. You are at risk also if you allow the deafness to take over your life. You can become consumed by it to the point that you do not develop other aspects of your life that are allowed to wither as you pursue the elusive goal of turning out the perfect deaf child. The paradox here is that, in order to do the parenting job well, you must also let go of your child and turn the deafness over to him or her. This becomes very difficult for the super-dedicated parent for whom the deafness is the focus of life. The letting-go that all parents must face becomes almost impossible to accomplish because if you are not a parent of a deaf child, who are you?

Guilt-driven parents often are also overprotective parents. The reasoning, as in the super-dedicated parents, goes something like this: "I let something bad happen to you once: I'm not about to let something bad happen to you again." It is always a tough call trying to decide what is overprotection and what is the normal concern of all parents for the health and safety of their child. There are also the special concerns that a parent of a deaf child must have. Research has shown, and my experience corroborates it, that parents of deaf children are less inclined to allow the children to explore on their own and to have as much freedom as normally hearing children. Overprotecting a child leads to a fearful, low-risk adult who passively accepts things. The message you are sending the child is that the world is not safe and that he or she is not competent, both of which may be true, but, if incorporated fully into the child's psyche, will lead to a self-limiting adult. The challenge for all parents is how to keep enough control to protect the child while at the same time allowing him or her to gain confidence in his or her ability to master the world. This will be discussed in more detail in the next chapter.

Overprotection also arises from the recognition of your vulnerability. All of us are vulnerable to the world—the truth is that we are naked and alone in the face of an indifferent universe. In order to protect ourselves from that uncomfortable truth we cloak ourselves in a myth of invulnerability. We think somehow that we will be able to dodge the bullet and someone else will fall, i.e., "bad things only happen to someone else." When a bad thing does happen, such as having a deaf child, then you realize what you really knew all along: that life is very fragile and that no one gets through life unscathed. Our children and all our loved ones are on loan to us, and that loan can be called in at any time. This realization at first leaves you scared, and you want very much to protect yourself and your child. A mother whose normally hearing twelve-month-old child was deafened from meningitis said:

> "When I got her home from the hospital, I wouldn't go out of the house with her. I kept her in for three months and would

not let any other child near her. When I finally took her shopping with me, I would spray the shopping cart with disinfectant before I put her in."

Although the recognition of vulnerability often leaves you fearful, it also can become a powerful impetus to living more authentically. Most people swim on the surface of their lives: deafness is also an opportunity to plunge into the depths of life.

The mother of the deaf child described above had this to say later on:

> "It [the deafness] made you more aware of things, more appreciative. It made me kind of stop and smell the flowers a lot more than I would before. I was always kind of rushing around and hurrying and not stopping—stopping as much as I do now because you just realize, I don't know, maybe your vulnerability. Who knows what is going to happen next? So you might as well enjoy now. I used to think that could never happen to me. But I don't feel that way anymore. Not in a real pessimistic kind of thing, but it is life and you have no control over it, so you might as well appreciate what you have, make the best of it."

The pain of deafness, the sense of loss, really never disappear. They become, in time, feelings of melancholy. A father of a deaf child once said, "At first it hurts like hell, then it becomes a dull ache that doesn't go away." Even for veteran parents of a deaf child, the initial pain often comes back again momentarily as life and events conspire to remind you and your child of the loss that deafness is. You find yourself often wondering as you look at your adult deaf child how it might have been if he or she were not deaf—the tears then may return.

Your feelings evoked by deafness always are strong, and at times they seem very negative. There also is good in deafness but it is hard to see, especially in the beginning. I am struck, as I watch parents go through the process of coming to grips with a deaf child, by how much joy and growth are involved. There is the joy you experience when your child reaches the milestone that you worked so hard to achieve. (Can there be any joy to match that of getting the first word?) Parents of deaf children are rarely in neutral: they are polarized on extremes of joy and despair.

As you are given permission by professionals and your family to have your feelings and allowed to work them through, marvelous transformations can take place. Confusion gives way to knowledge, anger becomes the energy to make changes, and guilt becomes commitment. The renewed awareness of vulnerability, when accepted, becomes an opportunity to restructure your priorities to find out what really is important in life.

There is a tremendous amount of growth in the process of raising a deaf child. We tend to give to life what life demands of us. Deafness is an opportunity to find that which is latent in us all but does not emerge until we are stressed. Deafness is a powerful teacher. A mother of an adolescent deaf child said:

> "Having a deaf child was the best thing that ever happened to me. I wish it were some other way but I have learned so much; I value myself so much more. I was becoming a housewife worried about the cleanliness of my home and what the neighbors were thinking. I now know how superficial that life would be and ultimately how unsatisfying for me. I am now on the school committee of my town, and I feel now that my life has both direction and purpose."

There is nothing in deafness that precludes the child from having a long, happy, and productive life; in fact, it may enhance the possibility. I am constantly reminded of the Bertrand Russell quote:

> To be without some of the things you want is an indispensable ingredient of happiness.

Happiness, say the poets, is a matter of having something to do, someone to love, and something to hope for. Deafness gives you all of this in full measure.

At the very least, this child has ensured that you will have an interesting life.

CHAPTER 2

The Parenting Process

Parenting is probably the hardest job I have had in my life. I know of no one who has done it entirely to his or her satisfaction. It is also one of the most rewarding occupations, but the rewards are subtle and always intangible. The joys of parenting are so intangible, and the stress and loss so obvious, that one wonders why anyone would want to have a child. Probably the nicest thing ever said to me—and I have had a lot of nice things said to me—was said by my youngest son when I dropped him off at college. He said, "You did a great job, Dad." I carry that remark with me always and I take it out and treasure it, especially at those all-too-frequent times when I feel like a failure as a parent. Being a parent is a very humbling experience!

Being the parent of a deaf child is an even more complicated experience. The deafness forces you to be more mindful of the parenting process and the ramifications of each decision you make. The task of parenting a deaf child is not qualitatively different from that of parenting a normal hearing child, only it demands more thought and care than we ordinarily give to the process when the child hears normally. It demands much more energy than parenting a hearing child: I know of no more exhausting "occupation" than caring for a young deaf child.

Parents of deaf children often needlessly burden themselves with the myth of fragility: the feeling that because the child is deaf, he or she is so fragile that the parents cannot afford to make a mistake. Deaf children are not nearly as fragile as parents assume and they survive and even grow from their mistakes. As parents, there is no way that you are not going to make mistakes—they are inherent in the process. Being a parent is at best a fly-by-the-seat-of-the-pants task that often must be invented as we go along. We can't make the correct decisions at all times, but we have the responsibility to monitor our decisions and to correct those that prove to be faulty. Children can accept and grow from almost anything except our indifference.

The goal of parenting any child, hearing or not, is to create an independent adult. We fail our children if, when they achieve maturity, they still need us. Parenting is a painful process because in order to succeed we must do ourselves out of a job. For the adult, there are no mothers and fathers, just brothers and sisters.

In order to achieve satisfactory adulthood we need to satisfy our psychological needs as well as our physical ones. Shutz, a psychologist writing several years ago, suggested that there is a hierarchy of human psychological needs beyond the obvious needs for shelter, food, and procreation. He proposed that humans need affiliation, affection, and control. Affiliation is the sense of belonging; the opposite of this would be alienation. Affection is the feeling of being valued; the opposite of this would be the feeling of worthlessness. Control is the sense of personal power, the ability to effect events to promote our own best interests; the opposite of this would be powerlessness. I have found the notions of affiliation, affection, and control useful ways of looking at children's developmental tasks, and the problems parents face when helping children negotiate these tasks.

Combined, they also become a useful model for looking at some of the special problems unique to raising a deaf child. All children must successfully navigate these issues in order to gain satisfactory adulthood.

AFFILIATION

Affiliation for the hearing infant is almost completely with the primary caregiver, usually the mother. There is evidence that the very young infant is unable to differentiate his or her body from the mother's body. As the child matures, the affiliation constantly broadens; the movement is always outward from the family. The preschool child identifies with the whole family as opposed to the infant-mother bond. Fathers and siblings become increasingly important figures in the child's life.

The school-age child broadens the affiliation even further At this point, the child usually is active in many different organizations associated with church, school, and/or community. I remember feeling resentment when I had to ferry my children to so many different activities—just like an unpaid and unappreciated taxi driver. It wasn't until my oldest child left home that I realized active parenting was all so very transitory, then I began to relax and enjoy the contact afforded by being in the car with my other children. Some of the best conversations I've had with my children have been in the car as we were going from one of their activities to another; they were a captive audience and I could philosophize at will.

Adolescence is a very difficult time for both the child and the parents, in part because the affiliation issue emerges very strongly: peers now have more power than parents to influence the child's behavior. Adolescence is not a biological phenomenon but rather a cultural issue that reflects the affluence of a society. The biology is rather simple: one day you are a child and the next, you are able to have children. Biologically, there is no protracted period of quasi-adulthood as there is in our cultural adolescence. We do not know much about adolescence, because it is a relatively new phenomenon reflecting the affluence of our culture and society. Poor families and marginal societies cannot afford to have adolescent children, a potential workforce, idle for years, so at age twelve or thirteen, their youngsters go through a rite of passage and become adults, rapidly assuming adult responsibilities. My father, the child of immigrant parents, never had an adolescence. He left school at eighth grade to work and support his family having forgone his own adolescence; consequently he did not know what to do with mine (neither did I).

As a society, we lack rites of passage that demarcate the passage to adulthood (probably the closest we come to it is in graduations); consequently, there is no warning bell for the parent, announcing the arrival of adolescence. It occurs when the child's peer group assumes much more power than the family to influence the child's behavior. In my family, the arrival was marked when my junior-high-school-age daughter was in tears every morning, afraid to go to school because she "didn't have the right clothes." Frustrated, I would respond, "Tell me which girl has the right clothes and we will call her up and find out what she is wearing." This was never answered and I envisioned parents all over town equally frustrated, wondering which girl was the trendsetter—we would find out and then we would assassinate her!

In order to start making the break from the family, the teenager needs to look critically at his or her parents and find them wanting. There is nothing a parent can do with teen-age children that does not embarrass them acutely. When my last child was thirteen, knowing what was coming, I took the summer off and we spent considerable time together. At fourteen, he would "play" with me if he couldn't find a friend; at fifteen, he wouldn't be seen dead with me. The only way I could take him to an activity was to purchase three tickets, the extra one for his friend. I think he was hoping that people would think I was the friend's father, rather than his.

Adolescents are also working hard on differentiation from the family, especially from the same sex parent, and establishing themselves as persons in their own right. At this period, if you say white, they say black. My oldest son, for example, tried very hard to be differentiated from me. I am a vegetarian who appreciates healthy foods. One day my son announced that he "liked the taste of preservatives." "What do they taste like?" I asked. "I don't know but I like them," was his response. Such is the level of dialogue one has with an adolescent!

The only way to survive your adolescent child is to keep a sense of humor. The final separation from the family is very difficult for everyone. My oldest daughter would often pick a fight before any prolonged separation. For her, it was easier to leave angry than sad. Unfortunately, she had to make several passes at leaving home, which made it very unpleasant for her mother and me. The whole process of leave-taking is very complex. I once attended a lecture by an eminent psychologist who was talking about the "Perfect Parent." According to him, "perfect parents" would be so sensitive to the adolescents' fear of leaving home that they would make life very uncomfortable for the children, so it would be easy for them to leave. I rushed home to tell my wife the news, and she assured me that I had nothing to worry about.

Affiliation for the Deaf Child

Affiliation for the deaf child is the same as for the hearing child. Deaf infants and young children generally identify themselves closely with their family of origin, and they rarely notice any difference between themselves and the rest of the family. If they do notice that their parents and siblings are not wearing hearing aids, it is usually passed over lightly. Later on (at about age ten or eleven), the difference becomes more noted and tinged with elements of negativity. How this is treated and how it emerges depends on how the parents feel about deafness, and on the child's school placement.

The awareness of difference usually emerges with the dreaded question "What caused me to be deaf?" Many parents tend to "hear" this question through the filter of their guilt feelings as though the child were asking "What did you do to cause *me* to be deaf?" and consequently they respond very defensively. Most children asking that question are becoming aware of their differences and there is not any blame or anger in the question. The child needs information, given impartially, and then to be listened to. This is usually the marker for when the child begins to equate deafness with being deficient.

Deaf children in mainstreamed situations generally will note the difference between themselves and their families much sooner than children in schools for the deaf. If they are struggling to keep up with their hearing peers, they often associate their problems with their deafness. Congenitally deaf children are not aware that they have a problem. For them, the world is as they've always known it. They do not know what it is like to hear. The "problem" emerges when they are asked to compete with hearing children and they fall short—they then see deafness as a problem that lowers their self-esteem and casts them adrift looking for a group to affiliate with.

For the deaf child, affiliation is an extremely complex issue, because over ninety percent of all deaf children have hearing parents. This means that the deaf child can form an affiliation with either of two groups that, at this point, are fairly disparate. Several writers have compared the present state of social consciousness of the deaf community with other minority groups, such as blacks and women. Many of the deaf community are "antihearing" in the same way that the black movement, in its early phases, seemed antiwhite and the women's movement, antimen. The dilemma here, for the hearing parents of deaf children, is that they cannot and do not belong to their child's minority group. Very often the parents are excluded from the deaf community and there is a pervasive fear among hearing parents that they are going to lose their child to the deafness. One mother of a young deaf child commented that she felt members of the deaf community were like a cult, waiting to snatch her child away. However, recognition and acceptance of the child's deafness and, consequently, of his or her possible place within the deaf community must be dealt with.

For deaf adolescents, affiliation is always an acute issue. It is often difficult for deaf adolescents to relate to their hearing peers, no matter how orally successful they may be. For example, they may be excluded from much of the social life of hearing adolescents which revolves around the telephone; things have gotten better for deaf adolescents with access to a TTY and parents of mainstreamed deaf children would do well to purchase several units that their child can lend to friends to facilitate communication with their hearing peers. E mail has also made a big difference. Despite technical advances, however, it is a rare hearing adolescent who will "put up with" the problems of having a deaf friend. Very often mainstreamed deaf children have few, if any, friends. No matter how adept the deaf child is, there will still be areas in which he or she will not be able to perform up to the level of hearing peers. The deaf adolescent in a mainstream situation can be very lonely and begin to cast about for a peer group; the deaf community becomes an attractive alternative to the loneliness of trying to integrate into hearing society.

It is at this point that hearing parents often become increasingly disturbed at the thought of "losing" their child to the deaf community. This is really a false problem. I do not think that any parents, whether they have a hearing child or a deaf child, can ever truly enter their child's world, nor should they. I do not know my children's friends or really know how they spend their time. My experiences of growing up and of being a young adult really do not apply to them; the world is so complex and fast moving that my children's growing up has been much different from mine. And I, in many respects, am a stranger to their world. The generation gap is a very real one, but this chasm does not necessarily impair my relationship with my children. We can, and do, share our experiences of family and caring for one another, and we will always have a special relationship but, in the end, we must all go our separate ways.

AFFECTION

Human beings require affection in order to survive. It has been shown that infants in orphanages failed to thrive when cared for by attendants who changed their diapers and physically cared for them but did not take the time to play with and fondle them. When the infants were given love and affection, they grew. This is true for all of us. We desperately need to feel loved and cared for—it is fundamental to our survival.

Unfortunately, because love is so fundamental to our happiness, it is often used as the major means to control children's behavior. The threat of withdrawal of love becomes a powerful control on a child's behavior. About the time a child is two years old, we begin to send him or her "I will love you if . . ." messages. "I will love you if you toilet train," "I will love you if you conform," and so forth. The obverse of this are all the "good boy/good girl" messages we send. The end result of this kind of control is that the child's view of self becomes dependent upon performance. The child incorporates the good boy/good girl message into "I am a good person if I please my parents." When this happens, the child becomes uncertain if the parents love him or her or love his or her performances. So much of the child's self-esteem gets tied to the performance that he or she cannot see that it is possible to be a smart, worthwhile person who sometimes does a dumb thing—or that he or she can be a good person and sometimes feel and act hateful. Parents always need to differentiate the child's behavior from the child, so they can dislike what the child did, and still love the child—not easy to do and not easy to communicate to the child. I always like to see parents with newborn babies—then their love is unconditional! The baby does not have to do anything, and he or she is adored. Unfortunately, most of us get such unconditional regard from our parents only for a very short time. (Grandparents become the source of the unconditional regard that parents do not provide—more on this in the next chapter.)

For the adolescent, performance becomes very much tied to self-esteem. Unfortunately, in a competitive environment, there can be only one winner and lots of losers, and so we tend to create a generation of adults who feel very insecure. These are the fathers who ask, "Do they love me for me or for my paycheck?" and the mothers who are always wondering whether their children and husbands love them for themselves or for all the things that they do. It is absolutely fundamental to our self-esteem to recognize that we're loved for ourselves. In order to do this we must give evidence of our love to our children and spouses when they are in neutral. A hug and expression of love are worth so much more when they are spontaneous and the recipient has done nothing to earn them, other than merely being.

Emotionally insecure parents usually produce insecure, low self-esteem children and perpetuate the cycle of adults who feel unloved and have low self-esteem.

Affection for the Deaf Child

The affection issue is an acute one for deaf children because the affection they receive frequently becomes a function of how well they are overcoming the disability of deafness, as seen by the parents. The deaf child very often has to carry the freight of the parents' anxieties about deafness and their own self-esteem. Parents frequently measure their success by the success of the child. This is true to a certain extent for all parents and all children, but it is especially true for the parents of deaf children. The deafness becomes a challenge to the parent as something to be overcome. The extent to which the child succeeds in being oral (and thus like the parents) is the extent to which the hearing parent feels gratified and successful. The deaf child has a whole area of performance to contend with that a hearing child does not have to face—namely, the speech and language area—and failure to meet parental expectations is often seen, by the deaf child, as causing a withdrawal of love.This is a major cause of the anger currently seen in the deaf community. Some members of that community have chosen to stop trying to perform according to hearing standards and have asserted their pride in sign language and deaf culture.

The time of diagnosis is a very difficult one for both parents and children. One mother of a newly diagnosed deaf child said, "For the next two months, I could barely look at my child without bursting into tears. It took me a long time to become natural and relaxed in my mothering." The emotional upheaval on the parents' part interferes with the natural bonding that needs to occur between parent and child. There is a professional push these days for early diagnosis of deafness, and while I agree that it is desirable to have a child diagnosed as soon as the parents begin to suspect a hearing loss, I am not convinced it is in the best interests of the child and the parents to have an intrusive diagnosis when there is no parental suspicion of a problem. Parents and children need that carefree time to bond without the fear and anxiety that would be introduced by professional suspicion of deafness. This is not wasted time—this is valuable time for establishing the child's self-esteem and the feeling that the world is a safe and caring place. Newborn screening, with its emphasis on very early detection, does not give parents or the child the luxury of enjoying one another, and may very well interfere with the bonding process that takes place early in the infant's life.

Parents who diagnosed their child's deafness somewhat later than did other parents in our group often expressed feelings of guilt that they wasted time. I think this guilt is unnecessary—it was time well spent. There is no evidence in the literature indicating that children with an early diagnosis do any better than children with a somewhat later diagnosis.

Adolescence is the time when the results of the parents' efforts become apparent. Up until this age, parents see their child as a potential success in terms of overcoming obstacles created by deafness. Parents who have been buoyed by unrealistic expectations and dreams are often disappointed when they realize that their dreams will not materialize. The adolescent deaf child often senses parental disappointment and responds by withdrawing. The deaf community becomes an increasingly more attractive alternative for the child. Communication between parent and the adolescent deaf child, which is always difficult, may now become almost impossible.

Parents must come to accept their child as being deaf and not as the super deaf child they had envisioned. The must also come to "love the deafness," as hard as that may seem. At issue for the parent is whether or not you cry about your child's deafness in their presence, i.e., whether you share your pain with your child. I think it is always psychologically healthy to share feelings openly within a family and it must be made clear to the child that your pain is about the deafness and not about the child. This is always very hard for the child to see. The deafness is very much a part of the child, and the child needs to feel loved in entirety. One cannot hate a part of oneself and become an adult with high self-esteem.

CONTROL

One of the most difficult issues of parenting is control—this issue occurs throughout the parenting process.

The task of the parent is to give the child control of, and therefore responsibility for, his or her own life a little bit at a time. The child is probably a bit more capable than the parent thinks and a bit less capable than the child thinks. This sometimes gives parents a very small margin to work in. The trick is the timing of relinquishing control. The timing must be precise. Parents must allow their children enough freedom to explore and grow; at the same time, they must maintain enough control so that the child is not injured. Parents who fail to allow the child enough control send a message that they don't think the child is competent enough to deal with a very dangerous world. Parents who allow their child too much freedom too soon may expose that child to many negative experiences, and the child may conclude on his or her own that he or she is incompetent in a very dangerous world. In either case, allowing too much freedom or taking too much control can result in a child who avoids risk and has low self-esteem. Often, parents must tread a thin line and it is a judgment call each parent must make.

Because of the control issue, raising any child is very much like warfare. Like any good general, you must pick your battles carefully. First, decide that the issue is an important one (health and safety are never compromised), and then be sure that it is a fight you can win. You cannot, for example, make a child talk.

Infants have minimal control of their world. Fortunately, infants have minimal needs. The infant cries and the parent changes a diaper or provides food; usually that solves the problem. If neither works, one finds a very frustrated parent and a very frustrated child. As the child gains more motor ability, he or she can control the physical environment. The principal means of control of the environment is through speech and language. By talking, the child makes demands on the parents.

As the child grows, the parent must allow more freedom; invariably, there is a lag between the parents' perception of the child's abilities and the child's own perception. Therein lies the inherent conflict between parent and child. The child's biological mandate is to grow and expand, which means testing limits. The parent's task is to restrict the child in order to guide and protect him or her. Eventually, the parent must give ground grudgingly and allow the child increasing amounts of freedom.

I see the conflict between parent and child as both necessary and desirable. Freedom cannot be given; it must be won. The inevitable conflicts between parents and children teach the children to respond to their own perception of reality, to learn to trust themselves and not to trust authority blindly.

At times, I think how nice it would be to have docile children, but then I remember soldiers who, following orders, killed their prisoners, and I think that we, as a society, are much better off creating adults who can and do think for themselves, who question authority, and who can and do take responsibility for the choices they make. As parents, we must encourage our children to think for themselves. Making choices and taking responsibility for those choices must be taught to a child very early. Parents need to control the universe of choices but, within the allowed sphere, respect the choices the child makes. For example, I was walking with my oldest child (then about three years old) and, getting tired, I said to her, "Why don't you sit down?" At this time in her life, control was a big issue, and she said, "No." My wife, alongside me, turned to her and said, "Alison, which chair are you going to sit on, the red chair or the blue one?" This solved the impasse. Alison had choices and we had established a universe of possibilities that we could live with. In the same vein, we saved many a fight by laying out three or four dresses that she could wear for the day. Of course, then she wanted to wear one that wasn't available, but that was another story.

Children also have to see that their own behavior has logical consequences. For example, if they spill milk, then they must clean it up; if they come home late, then there won't be time to watch their favorite TV program. Ideally, the parent is not the punishing agent—the child punishes himself or herself. This is not always possible to do: where health and safety issues are concerned or core family values are at stake, parents have to step in quickly and decisively. There are issues that are not negotiable.

The control issue is a constant dilemma for parents. Parents have gained wisdom from having made their own mistakes and want to save their children from making the same errors. To do this would keep the child a child for the rest of his or her life. We learn from our mistakes and we learn from adversity. It prepares us for the inevitable losses we must experience. A perfect childhood is not one in which there is no failure and no adversity—that is a myth that does not prepare a child adequately for the adult experience. One of the hardest things any parent has to do is to allow the child to make his or her own mistakes.I have decided that raising children, especially adolescents, is essentially a religious experience. I found myself praying a great deal when my children have gone off to do what I considered to be dangerous things. They, in their naiveté, could not see the potential danger in, for example, going to the prom with a date who just got his driver's license—sometimes you have to bite the bullet. To be successful as a parent, you not only have to be good, you have to be lucky, too. Sometimes perfectly good kids from good homes are just in the wrong place at the wrong time and there is nothing you can do about it, except pray.

Making the judgment about allowing freedom is very difficult and must often be made spontaneously. I remember my oldest son at sixteen asking me if he could go to the movies. There must have been something in the way he stood that alerted my "father bell," the one that rings "Alarm, dangerous rapids approaching!" because this was an unusual request—he had been going to the moves regularly without asking permission. I asked him to tell me more about the movie he was going to see and it turned out it was X-rated. At that point, I wanted to stop the dialogue and call Dr. Spock for his advice, but I was pinned and had to make a decision. I told him that he could go, but that I wanted him to talk to me about it the next day. At breakfast, I asked him how the movie was, and he told me "boring," and we've never talked about it since. I don't offer this anecdote as a recommendation to allow sixteen-year-olds to go to X-rated movies, but as a reminder of how hard the parenting process is. We often have to make spot decisions that will affect our children's lives, and we get no feedback about whether or not we made the right decision. For example, did I give up too much control at that point? I don't know. I often have wished I could get a card in the mail telling me I had done the right thing.

Control for the Deaf Child

Parents (and teachers) of deaf children are most likely to fail in the area of control or, more specifically, in the area of assumption of responsibility. For one thing, because of unresolved feelings of guilt and vulnerability, there is a strong tendency to overprotect the child. One of the worst things an adult can do (grandparents are notorious for this) is to pity the deaf child and not hold him or her to the same standard of behavior and responsibility that you would a hearing child. A parent in one group said, "Having a deaf child is bad enough. Having a spoiled deaf child is impossible."

The dilemma for the parent is that there are areas in which the deaf child cannot be expected to perform as well as a hearing child or be allowed the same freedoms a hearing child might be accorded. For example, the mother of a three-year-old deaf child, afraid to let the child out of sight because he might get lost and can't speak well enough to tell people where he lives, faces the dilemma of seeming either to overprotect the child or to be irresponsible. Solutions generally can be found, but one has to be creative. An identification bracelet may be a good solution and following the child at discreet distances for a while until you can be sure he has developed "street smarts" might be a middle ground that would allow the child some necessary freedom and the parent some ease of mind. It is not always easy to find the middle ground between allowing the child freedom to grow and giving the parents peace of mind.

There is a convincing body of evidence that deaf children and deaf adults remain passive and fail to take responsibility for themselves. A recent survey of teachers and counselors at schools for the deaf asked them to rank, in order of importance, twenty-four social competencies that the students needed to develop. The number-one ranking, by far, was the need to accept responsibility for one's actions. This was brought home to me vividly when I was lecturing at a school for the deaf with a mixed audience of teachers and students. There was an interpreter behind me on the stage. After my lecture, which was on responsibility assumption, there was some time available for questions. A man in the back of the room angrily raised his hand. He was deaf and, through the process of reverse interpretation, said the interpreter was placed on the stage so the light was behind her and he couldn't see; therefore he missed the whole lecture. Obviously, at the beginning of my talk, he could have either moved his seat or asked to have the interpreter stand elsewhere. He did neither and waited for someone to rescue him from his dilemma. I think it very sad and very symptomatic that he had failed to learn that he has power and can make things happen in his best interests. I think he was taught a "learned helplessness" by his parents and his teachers. There are a great many people in this world who would rather grumble about the darkness than light a candle—unfortunately, too many of them are deaf.

TRAPS FOR PARENTS OF DEAF CHILDREN

Over the past thirty-five years of working with parents, several problems have emerged time and time again. I am not sure they are unique to deafness, because they seem to underlie any parenting process that requires a heavy concentration of parental time and energy and could be generally true of any special needs child.

Focusing on the Deafness to the Exclusion of the Child

A deaf child is, first and foremost, a child who happens not to hear well. I have met too many so-called "successful" deaf adults who are able to speak well and have some marvelous occupations that one does not ordinarily associate with deaf people. As I've gotten to know these people, I have found some of them to be rather miserable human beings with a limited capacity for joy and a limited ability to relate effectively to other people. To my mind, these people are failures. What good is oral success and vocational success if it brings no joy and no satisfaction in relationships? I think this loss can come about as a result of a too narrow focus on the deafness by the parents. If you ask parents to draw a picture of their child shortly after the diagnosis of deafness, they draw a small child with enormous ears. Their focus is so much on the deafness that they often exclude developmental needs at great risk to the child's over-all development. This can and does produce a distorted adult. (This trap is not confined to parents who use an oral approach; signing parents can also "lose" their child in the deafness.)

Focus on Child to the Exclusion of Family and Self

It is very easy to get "lost" in the deafness—it can become all-consuming for parents. (Usually it is one parent who becomes super-dedicated, trying to work off guilt feelings.) There are only twenty-four hours in a day and seven days in a week; if a great deal of time and energy is being spent on the deafness, then something else has to go. This might be time that would be devoted to siblings and, very often, time devoted to the marriage. I have seen too many siblings at risk because of a lack of attention (more on this in the next chapter), and I have seen many marriages founder. Deafness in a child does not cause divorce; it does cause stress on the marital relationship. Cracks that originally could be papered over may appear in an already weak foundation. Stress caused by deafness becomes the catalyst for the split. Over-involved parents sometimes reflect a bad marriage. They are trying to get something, usually intimacy, from the their parenting that they are not getting from their marital relationship. Often an otherwise good marriage can be stressed beyond the limits of endurance and founder for lack of attention and energy. Marriages have to be maintained constantly in order to grow; they die from neglect.

The obverse is also true. Some marriages seem to prosper from the stress. Deafness can pull a family together, and wives often discover latent caring and devotion in their husbands, while husbands discover and marvel at the strengths their wives demonstrate in the face of the stress caused by deafness. How the marriage comes through the stress of the child's deafness will depend upon how sound it was to begin with and how well the parents were able to communicate with each other.

The people who usually get "lasts" in the family are the parents themselves (invariably, the mother). This is always a mistake: a martyred, exhausted, resentful mother seldom does a good job. In order to be giving in any relationship, one has to be getting from somewhere else. You have to fill your "tank" periodically so you have something to give to your child. I fly frequently and I am always struck by the advice given to me by the stewardess. She tells me that if I am traveling with a child and oxygen is needed, I should put the oxygen mask over my face first. If I don't put the mask over my face first, I am liable to lose consciousness and than I would not be able to help my child. This is a powerful metaphor for parenting a deaf child: you cannot be helpful unless you have taken good care of yourself first. If there is one thing I have learned over the past thirty-five years, it is that happy parents turn out marvelous kids.

Over-involved parents also find it very hard to let go of their child, as all effective parents must do. It is very easy for a parent to define himself or herself in terms of the deaf child. When your identity is in the parenting, then "losing" the child means losing your role and commitment in life." If I am not a parent of a deaf child, who am I?" The "loss" of the child is so threatening that parents often unconsciously try to keep the child dependent. The mother of an eighteen-year old said:

> "When he left to go to Gallaudet, I wanted to pack my bags and go with him. I felt lost. For the first time in a long time, I had no P.T.A. meetings, no teachers to meet, and no medical or audiological evaluation to go to. I felt partly scared and partly free also. It was very strange."

There is always a void when a child leaves home. Parents of very young children must realize that active parenting is just one phase of the life cycle. I remember, when my children were two years old, wondering,"will it never end?" Now my oldest "child" is forty-two years old and I don't know how that happened. I feel that I slept late one morning and there she is, suddenly an adult. All during the process of raising children it is necessary to keep a part of yourself separate from the process, so that you are more than a parent (or a spouse, for that matter), so that there is something else in your life to fill the void when the child must leave.

Fathers Are Not Mothers, and Vice Versa

Each parent has a unique role in the raising of the child. Mothers tend to have a shorter-term focus and, by the nature of their day-to-day involvement, tend to be very much involved with health and safety issues. Because they have so much contact with the child, discipline is often a problem and it is very easy for mothers to become frayed by the interminable contact with their child. The child, too, seems to get jaded by seeing the mother all the time and becomes very excited when "Daddy is coming home."

Fathers usually have a more distant role in the child-rearing process. Their contact with the child is more limited and they are distracted often by occupational concerns. Their role in the family, usually, is to take a longer-range view of the deafness; they are generally less adept at day-to-day management of the child and less knowledgeable about the specifics of deafness management. For example, they are usually less adept at inserting the child's hearing aid than the mother is, and if the family has elected to sign to the child, less apt to be fluent in signing. Usually, however, they are better able to discipline the child than the mothers are, and their relationship with the child is less deafness-focused than is the mothers'. Fathers are more inclined to have fun with their child without recourse to lessons.

Mothers, at times, resent the feeling that the father is "cashing in" on their hard work and often want the father to respond to the child in the same way they do. This is always a mistake! Children do not need two mothers—parents are complementary to one another. You can have a disaster on your hands if everybody in the family is teaching the child all the time. Each parent must have a separate role. This is not to say they can't, at times, be flexible in their roles and certainly, they both must share responsibility for disciplining the child. At the same time, each must give what he and she can give uniquely to the child.

Mother as Family Intermediary

Mothers, because they are with the child so much and generally are most involved with the child's therapy, often are the one family member best able to communicate with the deaf child. While this is, at times, very gratifying, it also carries an enormous burden. Often everyone else in the family looks to the mother to explain what is going on in the family and to interpret conversations and TV programs. This can, and does, cause the mother to lose her traditional role in the family. She is so busy being the intermediary that she has little time to enjoy a conversation for herself or to just quietly watch a TV program. She can easily get lost in the interpreter role.

The solution is easy to suggest but hard to implement: some of the interpreting needs to be spread to other members of the family. It is also wise to back off occasionally and let family members founder a bit in trying to establish communication. I have found that, if left to their own devices, grandparents and grandchildren can usually communicate quite well even if it is not in the conventional way. Sometimes the parent, trying always to be the interpreter, interferes with the development of that unique communication system as both the grandparents and child become dependent on the mother to interpret for them. The same is true for other family members; difficulty in communicating can become the spur to their learning to sign.

Ultimately, we must turn over the deafness to the child—it is his or her responsibility to find a way to communicate with the world. Holding back from the intermediary role and allowing the child to founder a bit engenders the motivation to communicate. A bit of frustration is a good thing; it is an impetus to change. Too much frustration can turn a child off, so the parent has to be very sensitive to the frustration level of the child. My experience, borne out by the research literature, has been that parents of deaf children are too quick to intervene in the communication struggle of their children with others. When they do this, they tend to create a passive child always looking for an adult to interpret for him or her.

Parent as Teacher

All parents are teachers, whether they like it or not. For most parents, the teaching role is incidental to the parenting role. With a deaf child there is often a need to provide focused teaching. Because the deaf child (0–3 years old) has a limited amount of formal schooling, the parent (usually the mother) assumes an active and conscious teaching responsibility that can interfere with the parenting role. For example, parents of deaf children can forget to have fun with their child because they are so focused on "fixing" the deafness. Parents often are so frantic to get the word in and hear the child vocalize that they don't relax and simply enjoy their child. This is a great loss. The child does not need two teachers; he or she needs a parent and a teacher. Teaching can always be "bought"; parenting is not for sale.

A parent education program should heighten the good teaching that is incidental to good parenting; it should never try to make a "teacher" of the parent. Good teaching for a deaf child should be natural and unconscious.

Low Expectations

What has handicapped deaf people the most are the low expectations that parents and teachers have for them. The worst thing you can do to your child is to limit him or her because of the deafness. There has been an enormous underestimation of deaf children's ability. People (especially young children) conform to the expectations of others. If we, as parents, say, "My child won't be able to understand this or do this," invariably he or she *won't* be able to say or do this. What we must do is cause mild stress and frustration in our children. Stressed and frustrated people learn and grow; happy, contented people sit around all day contemplating their navels. While it is necessary at times to contemplate our navels, we also need to be seeking and growing; it is "the nature of the beast."

Looking for a Guru

There is a marvelous book that I commend both for its title and its content. The book is *If You Meet the Buddha on the Road, Kill Him!* It is written by psychologist, Sheldon Kopp. The title comes from an old Buddhist admonition that any Buddha that one meets on the road has to be a false one and, therefore, should be slain: the true Buddha is within each of us. As parents of a newly diagnosed deaf child, you are ignorant about many things pertaining to deafness. Why shouldn't you be? You need information that you will be getting from many different sources. Wisdom is knowing what to do with all the information that you have. You are the only one who possesses that wisdom. Each family is unique—you are an experiment of one and, while the experience of others is useful as a model, it does not necessarily apply to you and your unique situation. You must learn to trust yourself and trust your judgments.

Parents, especially in the early stages when they are feeling a great deal of anxiety, tend to want to find a savior—someone who will know the right answer and will make all the right decisions. There are many people who are very willing to tell you how to raise your child and how to make the right decisions; unfortunately, they are often contradictory.

A father said to me, "I want you to be the quarter-back on my team." When I declined, he offered me the position of coach, which I also declined. The only role I could play that would truly be helpful to him in the long term was as an enthusiastic, supportive, and knowledgeable fan.

If you follow a guru to avoid the struggle, you will not grow, and you will not have the opportunity to find that which is latent in all of us—our Buddha. Having a deaf child can operate like the irritant grain of sand in the oyster that fosters the production of a pearl. Without that sand, no pearl. I know that if you are willing to stay with the deafness and assume the responsibility by looking inward, wisdom and your own personal Buddha will be found.

CHAPTER 3

The Family

Family therapists tell us that the family is a system. This means that all the parts of the family are inextricably interrelated. One part of the system cannot be altered without every other part being affected. I have on my desk a cleverly engineered "toy." It is composed of five metal balls suspended by strings from a central bar. When you lift the first ball and let it fall, it hits the next ball and so on, so that eventually the last ball in line flies away from the line. In a simple way, the toy demonstrates how the energy in one part of the system is transferred to another seemingly remote part.

The toy is a very simple linear system; a family is a very complex one. Nevertheless, the principle of mutual effect is the same. When a deaf child is born into a family, everyone is affected, even seemingly remote grandparents. Most of the professional attention has been devoted to the deaf child, and, more or less, to the parents. There is very little research information or program support for grandparents or for siblings. Yet the impact on them of the presence of a deaf child in the family may be profound.

GRANDPARENTS

Grandparents are present in every family, whether or not they are involved actively. We always carry our family of origin into our new family. Our notions of what constitutes marriage and parenthood stem from our childhood experiences, when we observe and assess our parents' parenting and our parents' marriage. We carry that image with us when we start our new family, either by imitating our parents or by determining to be different (antiparent). In either case, we are influenced heavily by them. Only with time and thought do we begin to find our way into marital and parental roles based on our own direct experiences. Some of the change comes about in the initial phase of family formation, when the newlywed spouses first begin their family with their own ideas of what a family should be. Early conflicts in marriage are due to the stress of molding the spouses' different ideas of family into a new system; the system that emerges is based on and influenced by both sets of grandparents.

Grandparenthood is the ultimate phase of parenthood. It is being able to be a parent without having the responsibility. A grandparent can play with the child, enjoy him or her thoroughly, and then give the child back. Probably the one place that a child can have unconditional love is with grandparents. Grandparents' love is the kind of love born of patience, experience, and age; it is usually a quiet, undemanding love. It is rare that anyone has a poor relationship with a grandparent. Parents, because of their civilizing and instructing function, are often in conflict with their child. I always knew that if the police were on my tail, my parents would take me in, but they would believe the police. My grandmother would not only take me in, she would also believe me.

There is always a special relationship between grandparent and grandchild. A cynic has commented that grandparents and grandchildren are natural allies because they both have the same enemy. My son, the one who likes the taste of preservatives, has become a father. He now has a son and I know that his child, come adolescence, is going to hate the taste of preservatives (whatever they taste like), and will be my ally, giving his father a taste of his own medicine or, in this case, a taste of his own preservatives, which will bring to fruition the ultimate parental curse: "You should only have a child that does to you what you are doing to me!"

Unfortunately, grandparents seem to be rapidly disappearing as involved family members. In a recent survey, only fifteen percent of families reported an actively involved grandparent. Most families (70%) have grandparents who live far away and relate to the family only intermittently. This is a loss for the grandchild because grandparents, in addition to providing unconditional love, also serve as caregivers, as mediators between the parents and child, and as family historians. The changing role of grandparents is in part a reflection of our society's affluence. Grandparents became heavily involved in their child's family in most cases because they could not take care of themselves any longer. In fact, in many less affluent societies one of the main reasons for having children was to have them take care of the aged parent. (The other was to provide cheap labor.) Social security and pension plans have changed that, and now elderly parents can afford to live a vigorous old age far removed from their children, and they do so, in increasing numbers.

Everything being equal, the most involved grandparent is the mother's mother. There have been several studies supporting that finding. I know that is certainly true in my own family—my mother-in-law has been much more involved with our family than my own mother. In general, women find it harder to let go of their adult children, as they usually are more intimately involved in child rearing than are their husbands. Men are usually involved with occupational issues, so child rearing is not central to their lives, although I think this is beginning to change. The mother tends to want to redo her mothering (and sometimes her "wifing") through her daughter's children. She can identify with her daughter's life and does not feel competition, as she might with her daughter-in law if she were to become involved with her son's children.

Although grandparents may be marvelous for the grandchild, often they create a great deal more tension for the parents, and there is an inherent stress in the parent/grandparent relationship. The mother-in-law relationship is often difficult for families to negotiate, hence all the mother-in-law jokes.

A predictable life crisis occurs when we begin to realize that we really do know more than our parents. I am not referring to the adolescent experience as described so well by Mark Twain: "When I was fifteen, I thought my father was the stupidest creature on the face of the earth. When I was nineteen, I was surprised to find out how much he had learned in four short years." There is an adult crisis that we all experience when we realize that our parents are no longer there to protect us, that they are now beginning to look to us for answers and help. At first this may be very gratifying, a celebration of our adulthood; it is also frightening because we are now parenting our parents—there is no one protecting us anymore.

For many of us, this role reversal evolves over a long period of time, fueled by many small instances of our parents' increasing incompetence. This gives us a chance to grow into our role as parents of our parents. Having a deaf child forces the crisis to occur much sooner and much more precipitously than either the parents or the grandparents are ready for.

When we are hurting, we generally want and need support from our own parents. It is very disturbing to seek the help and find it is not there. Instead of giving solace, our parents are asking us for information and emotional support. This can, and often does, leave us feeling resentful and cheated: we want so badly to be parented at this time and instead find ourselves parenting our parents.

For the grandparents it is a double hurt, coming at a time in life when they are least prepared to cope with emotional emergencies. They are hurting for both their child and their grandchild. Grandparents, like most nonprofessionals, know very little about deafness, and consequently they must get the information second-hand from their children. Many find this hard to do. Grandparents' feelings parallel closely the parents' emotions. They feel grief, anger, guilt, anxiety, and confusion in varying proportions. They display their feelings in accordance with the cultural values of the family. More often than not, there is no openness about feelings between the grandparents and the parents— they usually are protective of each other, neither wanting to burden the other with pain. Unfortunately, this can be misinterpreted as indifference. Grandparents can be viewed, mistakenly, as cold and uninvolved when in reality they are frightened and concerned but very diffident about sharing their feelings. Parents and grandparents often need help in bridging the gap between them; without help, that gap often widens.

Parents are frequently not aware of how angry they are with their own parents. I often hear in parent groups an argument that goes something like this: "I know my mother cares, but she is terrified by John's hearing aid and she is afraid to put it in. We also sign to him but neither of them know sign, so I've decided not to leave him with them." I also hear parents say: "I just can't talk to my parents. Every time I do, they ask me if I have found a cure—my father keeps praying for a cure. They weigh me down!"

Our research indicates that grandparents stay locked in the denial stage much longer than do parents. They usually don't have day-to-day contact with the child or with professionals that would enable them to become knowledgeable about deafness and slowly to relinquish denial as an emotional crutch. Grandparents are frequently the loneliest people in the family. Parents usually get a chance to meet other parents, if not formally in support groups, then informally in waiting rooms and in meetings. Grandparents seldom have a chance to meet other grandparents and to share their unique perspective. In the Emerson program, every year we try to have a Grandparent's Day. Grandparent groups are the hardest groups to assemble because many grandparents live long distances from their grandchildren and visit only intermittently. We make the attempt every year by scheduling nursery on a Saturday, long in advance, and in the spring when grandparents are more likely to be visiting in New England. I really enjoy a grandparent group, not only because I am at a similar stage in my life, but also because I know how lonely they are and how much they need support from each other. It is a pleasure to be able to give so much help with the simple procedure of providing a support group.

Here are some of the things several different grandparents have said to me:

> "These were going to be our best years. My husband retired and we moved near our daughter. When we found out that

our grandson was deaf, it was like the roof fell in. For the first three months, we used to wake up each morning and cry. There has never been anything like this in our family ever. For the first few months, we could not even talk with our daughter. She was so sharp with me. There was so much anger. Now, it is better and she talked with me, but we are afraid that they are going to move to be near the school for the deaf and we will lose them again."

"I never could talk to my son about our granddaughter's deafness. He would always shut me out, even when he was a little boy. I know he is hurting and I can't talk with him."

"It is very frustrating to be so far away. I don't really know what is going on. Getting information on the phone is very unsatisfactory. I am confident my daughter can do this. She is very capable. I wish I could help her more."

"I feel so helpless. I don't know what to do. All I seem able to do these days is to say 'Poor me,' 'My poor children,' and 'My poor grandchild.' And I know that is not helpful to anybody."

"Our granddaughter's deafness has brought us together. My daughter has grown up so much in having to take care of this child. Frankly, I didn't think she could do it. She was always so immature. I really admire her now. She is a responsible woman who is coping well with a very difficult problem."

I feel strongly that grandparents can have a vital role to play in the family. The grandparent/grandchild relationship is such a special one that it seldom can be duplicated. (The closest may be the aunt and uncle relationships, which also have an unconditionality about them. The aunt and uncle are like young grandparents; unfortunately they seldom have the time to give to the child that the grandparent does.) I think in many cases it is harmful to deprive children of their grandparents, and even though the hearing aid may not get in or formal sign language may not be used, I have found that grandparents and grandchildren always find a way to communicate. Parents would do well not to interfere with that relationship.

As indicated in the last grandparent's comment, deafness in a child is not all bad for a family. Good can come from the crisis. Parents frequently come to discover, after they have worked through their pain and anger, that the grandparents are an important resource for them, although not in the way that they had originally expected.

Grandparents can provide necessary respite care by doing spot babysitting. They can also give a great deal of time and attention to the normally hearing sibling—attention that the parents cannot give because they are heavily engaged by the needs of the deaf child. More exciting for parents can be the restructured relationship with their own parents. For the first time parents can experience adulthood in relation to their parents and for the first time be treated by their parents as adults. While scary, this is also exhilarating.

SIBLINGS

Siblings are enormously important for the development of social skills. Within the sibling system children learn how to resolve conflicts and how to be supportive of one another. (They learn how to deal with authority in their relationships with their parents.) The sibling system teaches them how to make friends and allies, how to save face while losing, and how to achieve recognition for their skills. In the sibling world, children learn how to negotiate, cooperate, and compete. The "jockeying for position" within the family system shapes and molds children into their adult selves. When children come into contact with the world outside the family, they take with them the knowledge they gained from their siblings to form their peer relationships.

The sibling relationship is probably the longest lasting relationship of our lifetime. In some families this relationship is fostered and strong; in others, it is weak. Siblings serve to validate our growing up experiences. No two children are ever born into exactly the same family—the system is radically altered by the birth of each new child—but the closest person to share your upbringing with is your sibling. My brother is the only person I can talk to about certain growing up experiences because he shared them with me; we also gang up on our mother when her memory contradicts ours. (The world always looks very different to a child than it does to an adult.)

A topic that arises early in parent groups is the guilt the parents feel for not paying enough attention to the normally hearing siblings. Parents frequently are aware of the problem but don't have the energy or the emotional resources to deal with the sibling. Very often parents try to enlist the sibling as a therapist, which may have disastrous results.

Recently we conducted a study at Emerson College in which we interviewed in depth the siblings of deaf children.There is in the literature a comprehensive study of the siblings of retarded children. The results of these two studies, in addition to personal observations, show that the normal hearing sibling always is affected. The sibling who frequently is the least affected is the oldest male child, while the oldest female child is always the most affected. The affect can be both positive and negative; as with everything in deafness, it is not all bad.

Some of the negatives reported by the siblings were:

• A feeling of having been neglected by their parents. Feeling that they had to be super-good, that they could not afford to have a problem because their parents were so stressed from dealing with the deaf child's problems, that they had no strength (or time) to deal with the sibling's problems.

- Feeling guilty that they had normal hearing and their sibling did not. Almost all siblings I've talked to have felt some guilt that they managed to "escape" the deafness; although they may have felt gratitude, they also felt guilt. This is known in psychologic literature as Survivor Guilt. I think this is magnified when parents have different expectations for the hearing child than for the deaf child—expecting the hearing child to be "better" because he or she can hear. The siblings also felt guilt when they got angry with the deaf child. There is a mythology that invades families with a deaf child that this child is very fragile and therefore everybody, including the sibling, must treat him or her with kid gloves. So, in the ordinary course of sibling competition, when the normally hearing child might get angry and might even strike out at the deaf child, he or she also felt guilt.

- Shame at having a deaf sibling. This is especially true in adolescence when the child is so concerned about what other people are thinking. For many siblings it becomes very hard to sign in public because they feel they stand out in the crowd, or to introduce their deaf brother or sister to friends because his or her speech is so poor. In some families (and societies) deafness is a stigma representing a sin. The hearing sibling often feels the shame of the "sin."

- Anxiety about whether their own children will be born hearing impaired. Almost all siblings have this fear of a family taint that they are somehow carrying.

- Hearing siblings often feel that they have lost their childhood because they are asked to assume adult responsibilities much sooner than their peers. Not only do their parents enlist them as interpreters and tutors for the deaf child, but they are asked to be surrogate parents as well. I remember the younger sister of a deaf adolescent boy feeling embarrassed that she had to make phone calls for her brother to ask girls for dates. She also had to tutor him in math, despite the fact that she was two years behind him in school. (It must have been tough on him, too.)

• There is always a lot of tension introduced into the family by the presence of the deaf child. There is stress on the marriage and there is stress in the management of the child. This increased stress spills over into all aspects of family life, which the hearing siblings usually feel acutely: their family is different, and not always in desirable ways.

The following is a letter written to me by a sibling of a deaf child who was in our very first nursery group. I think the letter describes the sibling experience poignantly and accurately.

> Dear Dr. Luterman:
>
> I have been very busy this spring with work, my two special education classes that I am taking at the University of Hawaii, and the new group that I joined called "Sign Express." It is a group of about fifteen people that sign songs and put on performances to help educate others about sign language.
>
> I have a lot of feelings about Robert's deafness and how it has affected me. I have only told my mother some of my feelings because she gets upset or angry when I say how I felt when I was little. I don't know if it is because she thinks that I am saying that she was not a good mother to me, or why she gets upset.
>
> I think when I was little, I had very mixed feelings. I felt very jealous of Robert but I also felt very proud of him. I can remember feeling very neglected, because I always thought that he got all of the attention from everybody. Of course, now I realize that my mother had to work with him more and it was necessary, but I didn't understand that when I was little. I remember wishing that I was deaf for a while thinking that then I would get more attention. I remember wishing that I would get sick and have to go into the hospital so that

everyone would bring me presents and give me more attention. I even remember trying to break my arm by jumping out of my treehouse (which never happened). I have never told my mother any of this. But I never hated Robert. I guess the way I dealt with my jealousy was by deciding to work with deaf children when I grew up. I decided this ever since I used to go watch Robert at Emerson College through the one-way vision mirror with my mother. And here I am, a speech pathologist working at a school where the deaf total communication class is housed, and I love working with deaf kids (ages 5–12).

I also remember being very proud of Robert. I can remember going to his school plays at the school for the deaf and having tears come to my eyes when I watched him on stage. I remember wanting to be friends with his friends there. I also remember people saying mean things about deaf people in general, like they can't talk and they are all "deaf and dumb," and feeling so hurt and intimidated that I couldn't even stand up for deaf people. I usually just said nothing.

I guess Robert's deafness probably created a lot of extra tension in my parents' marriage. I remember my mother getting really upset about the taxis taking him to school, some school problems, and other things. I remember my father not wanting to or just not getting involved and my mother getting upset at him. I really never understood just how it affected my father but I know it was real hard on my mother. I never really noticed what affect Robert's deafness had on Lynda, Michael, or Nicole [siblings]. I didn't get along with Lynda, Michael, or Robert that much when I was little.

Now I am much closer to everyone in my family. Maybe it's because I live so far away. I am trying to learn to sign fluently. Robert prefers to sign now and doesn't associate with hearing people if he can help it. Last summer, when I went home for a visit, I played the card game *Uno* with Robert and his friends. At first I felt uncomfortable, but it was a lot of fun and I think that was the first time anyone in our family associated with him when he had his friends over. I wish I could spend more time with him and really get to know him. I have been able to get ahold of a TTY a few times and I love being able to talk to him over the phone. I always felt bad when I called home on holidays and could talk to everyone and then just be able to tell someone to say "hi" to Robert. I remember a couple of times he would get on the phone and say "hi" to me and then my mother would get on the phone and say "that was Robert," like I couldn't tell. I remember when we used to watch TV when we were little and Robert would always ask us what was going on in the show and we would get so irritated at him and tell him to wait for the commercials. I wish we knew how to sign then and be able to interpret for him so he could understand while the show was on. I have very strong feelings about total communication.

Robert has told me a lot about how he always felt left out and that makes me feel so sad for him because if we only used sign language he would have been more involved and would have known what was going on. But I realize that is a big issue that probably never will be solved.

Well, I guess I rambled on quite a bit. I hope that this information will be helpful to you. If you have any more questions, please feel free to write me. I'll be glad to help in any way possible. I would love to visit you the next time I get back to Boston and also visit the clinic at Emerson College. Thank you for asking my feelings.

Sincerely,

Sara Murphy

How often do we ask siblings how they feel? The hearing sibling frequently is taken for granted. Our research has shown that the siblings most at risk are the ones from small families and those who are within two years of age of the deaf child. Our research also indicates that the child of the same sex is also at risk, but I suspect this was a sampling bias because in our study we had more female deaf children and female siblings. My own feeling is that a female sibling is more apt to feel guilt and to be burdened by the parents with teaching and caregiving responsibilities than a male sibling, at all ages and in all family configurations. I think this a function of how girls are acculturated in our society.

The solution to the sibling problem is easy to grasp intellectually but very hard to implement practically.

Parents need to direct attention to the sibling as a person, not just as a vehicle to produce a well-functioning deaf child. Emotions must be shared within a family and siblings must be given a chance to discuss their feelings of anger and guilt. Siblings need to be incorporated into all discussions regarding their welfare. For example, if the family decides to move (i.e., to be near a school for the deaf), the sibling needs to be consulted. The hearing child needs to feel that his or her needs are also being considered, and that he or she has some control of the future and of the direction the family will take. Information about deafness and about therapy needs to be shared with the sibling. Children have a way of concocting negative scenarios for themselves when they have incomplete information. For example, one hearing sibling thought that his deaf brother was either going to have normal hearing when he became an adult or die, because he knew no adults with hearing aids.

Grandparents can be useful in assisting the parents with the hearing sibling, although sometimes they focus too much attention on the deaf child. No matter how one looks at it, the family will have less time for other activities when there is a deaf child involved. What the parents have to ensure is that they spend quality time with the hearing child. For example, my wife and I always tried to have a special day alone with each of our four children; we would do something together with only that child. It didn't have to be more than two or three days in a year, but that seemed to be enough for each child.

The effect of the deaf child on the siblings was not all bad. There were positives here, too. Some of the siblings felt that having a deaf child in the family brought the family closer together, that everybody pitched in and helped, and it was fun to see that they had participated in the progress. Most siblings felt that they had more compassion and a greater sensitivity to prejudice than their peers who did not have a handicapped sibling. For many of the siblings, the deaf child became the impetus for finding a vocational direction. It is no accident that Sara, who wrote me the letter, is a speech therapist working with deaf children, and that many teachers of the deaf and interpreters for the deaf are themselves hearing siblings of deaf children.

What is very clear is that the more open and comfortable parents are about deafness, the better the normally hearing child is able to adjust to it. Parental adjustment precedes sibling adjustment.

THE OPTIMALLY FUNCTIONING FAMILY

Family therapists, when they take time out from their clinical duties, speculate about what makes a family function optimally. They need to do this in order to establish goals for the dysfunctional families they work with. There are five characteristics of optimally functioning families that I have been able to glean from the literature.

Communication Among Family Members Is Clear and Direct

Anyone who has written about well-functioning families (or dysfunctional ones for that matter) looks at the communication patterns of the family members. Clear communication is by far the most important attribute of the optimally functioning family. This is not easy to achieve in practice. For the past several years, since I have been reading so heavily in the family literature, I have been studying (with dismay, I may add) the communication pattern in my own family. For example, my wife and mother-in-law speak in a code that, for thirty-odd years of trying, I was never quite able to crack. The hallmark of my mother-in-law's communication patterns was never, ever to ask directly for what she wanted. She hinted at things and then you were supposed to guess what it was she wanted: if she was getting into the car and commented that it was hot, that was really a request to put on the air conditioner; if she asked if you would like ice cream, that really meant she would like some—please ask her. Occasionally, my wife would announce that her mother was angry. "How do you know?" asked I, and my wife would respond, "You can tell by the way she holds her jaw and the way she bites her words out." If I confronted my mother-in-law about her anger, she might have responded with, "Well, why don't you think about what you did?" and that's as far as it went.

This unwillingness to be direct left us all very uncomfortable because we always were trying to guess what was in her head. I remember one time the three of us were returning from dinner at a friend's house, and my mother-in-law was in the back seat of the car extolling the hostess and her wonderful house. My wife, in the front seat, was getting angrier and angrier. When I got home I asked my wife why she was so angry and she said, "My mother was saying I was a poor housekeeper." I don't know whether that is what she was really saying or whether she was innocently praising the hostess, and we will never know, but it would be so much easier if we could trust the surface comments; it would allow us all to relax.

I, too, am guilty of not being direct. I could wake up one morning and decide I would like pasta for dinner that evening, only I didn't bother to tell my wife that. I figured that after forty-four years of marriage, she should be able to read my mind. So I would go off to work expecting to have a nice spaghetti dinner when I came home. Unfortunately, my wife's ESP was off that day and although there was a perfectly good dinner in place, it was not pasta! I got angry because I was disappointed yet I knew I couldn't be direct about this anger. So I held a trial in my head and because I was judge and jury, I found her guilty as charged! Now I would wait for her to do something untoward that ordinarily I would just ignore, like drop a cup or mess up the checkbook, and then I would ZAP her. It's not that I was angry about the cup or the checkbook; I was angry about the failed expectation around the pasta. These implicit expectations are what mess up relationships badly because they invariably lead to anger and disappointments. How much easier it would have been if I had told her I would like spaghetti that night and we could then have negotiated the issue. I might not have gotten it that night but I would have gotten it at some point soon, and that would have satisfied me.

I am just as guilty with my son. I might comment to him, as he is sitting in the living room watching television, that the grass is getting very high. Off I go to work expecting to find the grass cut; when I come home it isn't. When I accuse my son of not mowing the lawn he tells me I didn't ask him to, which is true. So then I ask him to cut it and he agrees. Five days later, it is still uncut and I get very angry and cut it myself. When I confront him again he says, "I was just going to do it." Now I have learned (it has taken me four children and a stack of child-rearing books), to tell him that I want the lawn mowed between now and 5:00 p.m. tomorrow. Of course, at five minutes to 5:00 p.m. tomorrow, he finally takes out the lawn mower and starts cutting the lawn. Still, it is so much easier when I am direct and clear in my communication.

To be fair, my mother also has some deviant communication patterns. She is the master of the hidden directive. By this I mean that when she seems to be giving you a choice, there really is not a choice—she wants you to choose what she would choose if she weren't trying to be so democratic. These are pseudochoices. If she asks me, "Which restaurant do you want to go to?" I know, after all these years, that the best answer for me to give is, "Which restaurant do you want me to go to?" and she'll tell me. When we get to the restaurant, I ask her, "Which dish do I want to order?" and she'll tell me. Before I got sophisticated, if I chose "wrong," she would convince me that I really wanted what she would have chosen. As stated in the previous chapter, it's the parents' job to set the universe of choices and then to respect the choice that the child ultimately makes. My mother apparently never read this chapter.

My mother is also President and Chief Operating Officer of the "Put on a sweater because I'm cold" club. (I understand it has international affiliates.) A conversation with her when we are sitting outside watching a Florida sunset might go like this: "David, put on a sweater; it's cold." First I would try to deal with this semantically. This is mistake number one. I would say, "Mom, instead of saying '*It's* cold,' why don't you say '*I'm* cold,' and then *you* go put on a sweater." She would look at me quizzically and say, "What's the matter with you? It's cold, so put on a sweater." Then I would try to deal with the content (mistake number two), and say to her, "Mom, I am past sixty. I am a college professor. I write books. I give lectures. Don't you think I know enough to put on a sweater when I'm cold?" Then she would say, "No," and then I put on the sweater, which is what I should have done in the first place. My mother has a hard time letting go being a mother.

It is not easy to keep the communication in a family direct and open; everyone in the family has to keep working at it all the time. It is well worth the effort; life in the family is so much easier when people are direct and clear.

In an Optimally Functioning Family, Roles and Responsibilities Are Clearly Designated, Overlapping, and Flexible

For a family to function, each member must pitch in and perform some duties that enable the family to function; somebody has to shop for groceries, someone cooks, someone cleans, someone puts out the garbage, and so forth. In an optimally functioning family, the roles are allocated on the basis of ability and time availability; in a less-than-optimally functioning family, the roles are allocated on some other basis, usually sex or age. Thus, the father gets the job of fixing things around the house because he is a man, and the mother cooks and cleans because she is a woman, despite the fact that he might be the better cook and she the better mechanic.

There also needs to be role overlap so that the family can function even if one member is not there. I remember when my mother had to go to the hospital for a week and my father, brother, and I were left to our own devices. We foundered badly, and if my grandmother had not come to take care of us, we might not have survived. To an outsider, it might look as if this was the fault of us men; in reality, it was my mother's doing: she had defined herself (she still does) as someone who takes care of her men. She would have been threatened if we learned her skills because that would mean that we could function without her. In an optimally functioning family, the roles overlap so that the mechanic husband can also cook and the "cook" wife can also repair an appliance.

Roles also need to be flexible so that they can be renegotiated. Children, as they get older need to assume more responsibilities; siblings need to trade off on their family chores. At different times in the family life cycle, members will be present or absent, capable or incapable; the family has to leave room to renegotiate the family roles as circumstances warrant.

Family Members Accept Limits for the Resolution of Conflict

In all healthy families, there is conflict. Growth and change come from conflict or, more accurately, growth stems from good conflict resolution. I did not appreciate this fact when growing up—I thought that an optimally functioning family had no conflict and that my family, who squabbled a great deal, was somehow dysfunctional. I see now that this was healthy. the parent-child relationship is inherently one that includes conflict: the parents' job is to restrict and civilize, while the child's job is to grow and test limits. Siblings are always in competition with each other and in competition for their parents' attention and affection. It is not the presence of conflict in a family that determines its health but rather how the conflicts are resolved.

In a healthy family, disputes are resolved in a way that is mutually satisfactory, always with a face-saving formula for any loser. Finding a satisfactory solution requires a great deal of thought and time. I remember once going on a picnic with a family from the nursery. It was a large family, and for dessert the mother produced a large cake. Two of her children proceeded to argue, each one claiming the other would get the bigger piece. The mother turned to one of the children, handed him the knife, and said, "Okay, you cut the cake and he'll (pointing to the brother) get the first piece. Next time we have a cake he'll cut and you will get the first piece." I have never seen a cake cut so evenly.

Children need to sense that solutions are fair and that individual needs are always considered. Conflicts are not resolved because one person is older or bigger than the other. Rather, each side is heard and a fair solution is proposed, which sometimes means that we have to defer what we want to a later time. People are willing to do this if they know that at some future time their wants will be considered first. Parents must model good conflict resolution skills for their children. Children need to see that adults in the family can get into a dispute and resolve it fairly. When that happens, everybody wins.

In an Optimally Functioning Family Intimacy Is Present and Is a Function of Frequent, Equal-powered Transactions

One of the basic functions of a family is to provide an environment where everyone feels loved. Family needs to be a place where we feel safe and cared for. To adapt the words of the poet—"Family in the place where they have to take you in." Different families have different ways of expressing their love. In my family, with its Middle European roots, we expressed love physically. I can remember big, sloppy kisses from grandparents and aunts and uncles. In other families, the expression of affection is much more subtle and not always apparent to an outsider. When I was in Australia staying with families, it struck me how little they touched one another. Then as I watched, I realized that they stood closer to family members than they did to nonfamily members. As you get more intimate with Australians, they let you move closer.

It is absolutely essential that children receive the affection message. Some of our angriest adolescents are the ones who feel unloved. We have strong species-wide needs to feel loved and affiliated with a unit; without this our survival is threatened.

There Is a Healthy Balance Between Change and Stability

Life is changing all the time. Children get older, parents age, and life has a way of throwing us some curve balls occasionally. A family must adjust to these changes while maintaining its stability, very much like a man on a highwire who oscillates back and forth as he goes across the wire in order to maintain his balance.

A dysfunctional family falls apart when it is stressed by an outside event. A deaf child is a severe blow to the family balance; roles have to be shifted and conflict always emerges. An optimally functioning family can absorb the blow and maintain its balance by making the necessary changes in order to "keep itself on the wire." It is easy to see that if there is indirect communication, role rigidity, poor conflict resolution skills, and not much affection, the family will founder. But, if the family is functioning optimally or close to optimally in its other attributes, i.e., if there is clear communication, role overlap and flexibility, good conflict resolution skills, and lots of affection, then the family will be able to grow and even flourish in the face of the crisis caused by the child's deafness.

It is hard work to maintain a family as an optimally functioning unit, and at times, we may wonder if it is worth the effort. However, our survival as a species on this planet is dependent on how well we function at the family level. Our individual survival depends for many years on our family because we are born helpless and dependent and we learn our important adult life-skills within the family context. In order for us as a society to move forward, we need to optimize the family. By creating adults who can love, negotiate, and communicate, we will advance our civilization. Each of us must bear some responsibility for this; our salvation as a species depends on our ability to improve our families—we must not perpetuate the sins of past generations.

CHAPTER 4

Coping

My dictionary defines coping as "contending successfully with." All coping involves a stressful interaction between a person and his or her environment. Coping is any response to a difficult life situation that avoids or prevents *distress*. Distress occurs in life when a person experiences too many external demands without having adequate control. When this happens, the individual eventually breaks down and fails to cope or, more accurately, the coping strategy becomes one of complete withdrawal.

With coping there is always the possibility of growth as there is a continual demand for change. When you are stressed by an external "problem," such as having a deaf child, you must come up with a new set of responses to contend with the changing set of external demands. Coping is a dynamic and continuous process. It is a moment-to-moment proposition. Coping with a deaf child is a long, ever-changing haul—you are always going to be required to come up with new sets of responses as the child grows and as circumstances change. This makes life with a deaf child unpredictable and almost always stressful. It is also very interesting.

COPING STRATEGIES

There are four general coping strategies. The first and perhaps the primary one is flight. The initial decision anyone must make in a stressful situation is whether to fight or to take flight. At times it is very appropriate to flee. There are some overwhelming situations one may meet for which "fight" would not be the appropriate response. The problem with flight as a coping strategy is that it leaves one vulnerable to guilt and invariably reduces self-esteem. It is hard to like oneself and be a "quitter" at the same time. Nevertheless, flight is at times a very appropriate response.

For some parents the stress of a deaf child is overwhelming and they opt to leave. There are little data on the effect of a deaf child on the divorce rate; my impression is that divorce in families with a deaf child parallels the appallingly high rate of divorce in the general population. It is not uncommon to find parents who have left their marriage and given up any responsibility for managing the deaf child; often the departing spouse will blame the deafness as the reason for leaving (he or she usually blames the spouse for spending too much time with the deaf child). My own feeling is that usually the marriage was weak to begin with and that the departing spouse could not have handled much stress at all without resorting to flight. There is no way we can live our lives, and especially raise children without encountering a great deal of stress. Some people are better equipped to cope with such stress than others.

All parents at times experience psychological flight. This can be as mild as a feeling of unreality or as threatening as fantasies of one's own death or the death of one's child. The death fantasies are the ultimate release from a very painful situation. In one sense the child has "died," at least the expected child, a child who could hear.

Fantasies about a child's death are very common, although seldom admitted or discussed. This "death wish" is in part due to the desire to make the problem go away, not the child necessarily, but the stress of the deafness. Because the problem is so painful, the "solution" is quite understandable. There is no need to feel guilt; fantasies, like feelings, just are—they are neither good nor bad and do not need to be judged, just accepted and acknowledged. Behavior can be judged as to whether or not it is helpful. The fantasies serve a very useful function of allowing psychological flight while, at the same time one is hanging in there and coping with the deafness.

The second coping strategy is to try to modify or ameliorate the deafness. Although the child will never (at least at this time because of lack of technology) be able to hear normally, there are things that can be done to minimize the handicapping effects of the deafness, such as getting the child appropriate amplification, finding suitable educational programs, and following through on prescribed medical and/or educational therapy. Doing these things gives us some control over the situation. The trick in trying to modify the stressful situation is in knowing what can be modified and doing it, and then learning to accept what cannot be changed—not always easy to do. To err is to be frustrated.

Concerning those elements of the situation that cannot be modified, the stress of deafness can be reduced by changing the way of looking at it. This is technically known as *cognitively neutralizing the stressor*—a mouthful that means it is all in the way that we choose to look at things. Our view of events determines the emotional intensity of our response.

Our glass can be either half empty or half full, depending on how we view the glass. We can feel very fortunate that we have a half glass of water, or very deprived that we have only a half empty glass. Probably the most frequently used cognitive neutralizer is a method known as *positive comparisons*. This is the "It could be much worse" strategy of coping, as in, "It could be worse—he could be retarded." (For parents of a retarded child it would be some other disability, and so goes it.) It is one that I hear very often in groups and that parents are frequently told by their friend and relatives—designed to make them feel better, but seldom successful, at least for any length of time. I don't particularly like this strategy, because it leaves one vulnerable to guilt when already feeling bad about having a hearing-impaired child. I don't know of any parent who at one time or another has not felt bad about having a deaf child. You are entitled to that pain; if you feel it could be worse, you then tend to feel that you should not be grieving about the deafness—after all, "He could be retarded." I don't think it is ever productive to feel guilty because you are grieving about your child's deafness.

Personally, I think there are more fruitful ways of neutralizing the deafness cognitively. I prefer to see it as a gift, as something you have been given. I see deafness as a powerful teacher for both the child and the parent. I think all deaf children come with this gift, admittedly one that is buried under a great deal of pain, but a gift nonetheless. I hope, in the course of raising your child, you can find the gift.

The fourth and last general strategy is to deal directly with the stress. We have a wide array of stress reducers available to us, and each individual must find his or her own. One mother I knew took long, hot baths, another would knit, while a third baked pies.

What is effective for one person may not work for another. One stress reducer that is almost universal is exercise. Exercise works as a stress reducer because it is always a time-out experience to get you away from the child and the deafness. It also has an emotionally calming effect, what psychologists refer to as a centering activity. Repetitive exercise such as jogging, swimming, or bicycling puts the mind into a meditative state. When I start out emotionally upset on my morning jog, I am almost always able to return in a much calmer state. Somehow, the problems seem to work out—I don't deliberately set out trying to solve problems, but jogging, for me, is a "moving meditation" and works very well in reducing the stress in my life; I know it is vital to my mental and physical well-being. Also, good physical condition is helpful when dealing with emotional stress. I have more energy and I am more in control when I am in good physical shape than when I am not.

These, then are the four general strategies of coping: flight, modification, cognitive neutralization, and stress reduction. Individuals can and do use any and all of these strategies at any given time; in a given situation, one strategy may be more effective than another. Following are some specific suggestions for coping with deafness in a child.

TAKING CARE OF ONESELF

You are the most important family member, although it is hard to see this when all of the energy in the family seems to be focused on the deaf child. If you are nonfunctional, the family becomes nonfunctional. There is a strong need for periodic time-outs. Coping with a deaf child is like running a marathon. One has to get in there and slug it out on a day-to-day basis. You are in for the long haul. I remember reading an article in a running magazine by a writer who was in the lead truck watching Bill Rogers set the record, at that time, for the Boston Marathon. Rogers, who was far ahead of the field, at one point stopped (which is unheard of in marathon circles), had a drink, and looked around. At another point he stopped and tied his shoe laces—and still went on to set a record pace for the distance. The writer at first thought that if Rogers hadn't stopped twice, he would have broken the record even further. Then, after considering it for a minute, he realized that maybe Rogers had set the record because he *had* stopped twice.

I think that's true for parents of deaf children. Every so often you must come up for air. In the Emerson program, we always give parents a "day off" once or twice a semester. We suggest to them that they drop their child off and leave for the morning without doing anything, including thinking about deafness. The parents usually come back from their morning off refreshed and eager to get back to work with their child.

SHORT-TERM FOCUS

If you think long term about all the things you will have to do and all the problems you will encounter, you can get very scared very easily. It is absolutely overwhelming. If you can keep a short-term, one-day-at-a-time focus, then the problems seem manageable; and if one day is too long a time span, then try an hour-to-hour span. There are days when you will need a very short-term focus to survive. It is also vital not to second guess yourself. When confronted with a need to make a change, you must marshal as many facts as possible, and then move ahead. Sometimes the decision you make and the course of action you take are not the most fruitful; then you change them without regrets. (It is really not a mistake. You have obtained valuable information. This is discussed in more detail in Chapter 7.) To allow yourself to wallow in "should/ oughts" is self-defeating. The lamented past and the unknown future are beyond you. Live more in the now and your problems are manageable. You have some control over what you do in your now; you will feel much better for that control.

TAKING AND GIVING RESPONSIBILITY

I have a sign over my bed: "It is their problem," and I look at it every morning. It has kept me sane in raising my children, especially as they approached adulthood. When children are young, all their problems are their parents'. As children grow, more and more responsibility must be vested in them until ultimately the children have all the responsibility and parents have little or none. This is the parental task. At all times you must be asking yourself, "Is this my problem or my child's problem?" My experience with parents of deaf children is that they assume too many of their child's problems and, therefore, impede their passage into adulthood. This is especially true when it comes to managing the deafness—it must be turned over to the child. For example, when you go to McDonald's, the child, at some point, must be encouraged to order his or her own hamburger, and pay for it. Later on he or she will have to earn the money to buy it. *When* to relinquish control is always the acute parental problem.

You are not deaf (at least ninety percent of deaf children have hearing parents), and the deafness is your child's problem, not yours. In the early years, it is your problem, and you must make the decisions (and live with them) regarding amplification and education. As your child matures, he or she must begin to make these decisions and must live with them. Distinguishing between what is your problem and what is your child's problem is a continuing dilemma of parenthood.

GETTING IT INTO PERSPECTIVE

When your child is first diagnosed, you live, sleep, and breathe deafness; it consumes and dominates your family and life. Almost all your waking thoughts, and many of your dreams, focus on the hearing loss in your child. But deafness is only one aspect of your child and only one aspect of your life—albeit an important one. Your child can and will do many things well, as well as any hearing child. Parents must learn to see the normality that is present both in their lives and in their child's.

BEING A PARENT, NOT A THERAPIST

All parents are teachers. You have a responsibility to guide and instruct your children, and there is no getting around it. Yet you are not the child's formal teacher. Parents of deaf children must be able to translate what they learn from the child's teacher to the home situation. They must create an atmosphere and an attitude that is conducive to living and learning. This should not involve formal lessons such as the teacher of the deaf provides, but rather it should be a blend of general acceptance and love that a home can provide with the intellectual stimulation that a school provides. A home is not a school and it should not be made into one.

I have found in my own life, which has been complicated greatly by my wife having multiple sclerosis, that my mental health and my ability to cope with many difficult situations are based on three cardinal rules: one, that I accept my feelings for what they are and only judge my behavior in terms of whether or not it accomplishes my goals; second, that I deal with my situation on a day-to-day basis; and last, that I focus on what I have, rather than on what I've lost. Another thing that has helped me has been trying to adhere to the "Ten Commandments" written by ninety-year-old Elodie Armstrong, who had multiple sclerosis for forty years. (I culled this from an Ann Landers' column, originally published in the Longview, WA *Daily News.*)

1. Thou shalt not worry, for worry is the most unproductive of all human activities.
2. Thou shalt not be fearful, for most of the things we fear never come to pass.
3. Thou shalt not cross bridges before you get to them, for no one has yet succeeded in accomplishing this.
4. Thou shall face each problem as it comes. You can handle only one at a time anyway.
5. Thou shalt not take problems to bed with you, for they make very poor bedfellows.
6. Thou shalt not borrow other people's problems; they can take better care of them than you can.
7. Thou shalt not try to relive yesterday for good or ill—it is gone. Concentrate on what is happening in your life today.
8. Thou shalt count thy blessings, never overlooking the small ones, for a lot of small blessings add up to a big one.

9. Thou shalt be a good listener, for only when you listen do you hear ideas different than your own. It is very hard to learn something new when you're talking.
10. Thou shalt not become bogged down by frustration, for ninety percent of it is rooted in self-pity and it will only interfere with positive action.

THE ACCEPTANCE PROCESS

There are four stages to the acceptance process: denial, resistance, affirmation, and acceptance.

In denial, while you may admit to yourself that you have a deaf child, you do not "own" deafness psychologically: it is something alien to you. You may refuse to accept the diagnosis or, more specifically, the notion that the deafness cannot be cured. You may embark on a search of a cure or for another authority who will refute the diagnosis. There is a great deal of strength in denial, built in large part on the fear of change and insecurity about your inability to cope successfully. There is psychological comfort in denial: at times it feels as if you will fall apart if you have to confront the deafness directly. Denial can be maintained for just so long, however, because it is constantly assaulted by the evidence of the disorder. It also can be maintained for only a short time before it begins to damage the child's welfare. For a while, though, it is a necessary and normal step in the process of coming to acceptance.

In the resistance stage, you acknowledge that there is something wrong with your child's hearing, but refuse to accept a negative outcome. You think of yourself as a special case. This is the pledge you make at 3 A.M. as you toss and turn in your bed when you say, "Okay, my child's deaf, but he or she is going to be a super deaf child; capable of lipreading in the dark and around corners. His or her speech will be so good that no one will know that my child is hearing impaired." My wife, shortly after being diagnosed as having multiple sclerosis, ran a 10K race, as much to prove to herself that she could still do it as to state that she was a special case. In the resistance stage, you still keep the deafness secret and you don't join any organization promoting help for deafness because it means acknowledging your problem to others.

In the acknowledgment stage, you come out of the closet. You are willing and, most of the time, eager to talk about deafness with others, to educate strangers and anyone else you may come in contact with. I often ask parents, "When you take a picture of your child, is the hearing aid in or out?" When you are in the denial/resistance phase of coping, the hearing aid is out. In the acknowledgment stage, the hearing aid is in and is seen as a vital part of your child's existence. In acknowledgment, deafness dominates your life. You feel consumed by it.

The fourth and final stage, adaptation or acceptance is characterized by putting the deafness into perspective. It is learning to live with it, not necessarily liking it but recognizing that beating deafness is a matter of living your life to the fullest in spite of it or maybe because of it. Acceptance is not devoid of grief; it is characterized by a sadness that no longer is immobilizing. In this stage, you are able to spend time and energy on other aspects of your life. You also find a new life-style with changed values. You have undergone a boundary experience of your view of life, and living is now very different. Your life will never be the same again, but it can be a good life nevertheless.

Going through the stages is not a simple linear progression. There are many fits and starts. When you are confronted with any change or unexpected obstacle, the process starts over again. Helen Featherstone, the mother of a severely disabled child, described this so well when she wrote:

But I am uncomfortable with most stage theories, they carry too heavy a freight of straight line progress; they also suggest an implausible final harmony. The actual progress is not linear, and often is bought at a high price in human suffering. In the vocabulary of stages, acceptance becomes a kind of high plateau, once out of reach, now firmly felt underfoot. Gone are the fears of self reproaches of yesterday and sighs for what might have been. Matter-of-fact realism guides our effort. Having struggled out of darkness we will not have to be afraid anymore. . . . Few parents reach, an emotional promised land; most have good days and bad days. Acceptance does not signify an end to pain—one cannot suffer a grievous loss without travail. Even when acceptance is won, there are still bad times.[2]

Individual families will vary in the degree and speed with which they come to acceptance. Some families never get there; they appear forever stuck in the denial/ resistance mode, which seems to be the only possible coping strategy for them. They are paralyzed in their fear. Others move through the process rapidly, seeming to skip stages. I think the key to successful adaptation lies in the self-confidence of the parents. When you feel secure in your ability to cope, it becomes easier for you to assume the psychological risk of giving up the pseudo-comfort of denial and assuming the responsibilities demanded by the acknowledgment and acceptance stages. When you feel less confident and less secure, denial and resistance become attractive alternatives.

THE SUCCESSFUL FAMILIES

There is research literature on what makes a family successful in the business of raising a special needs child. None of the research has been done with families of deaf children, but I think the results of these studies apply as well to the deaf population. The design of these studies was essentially the same. Professionals who worked with the families were asked to rate them as successful or unsuccessful. When there was unanimous agreement, the researchers interviewed family members in depth. Four characteristics stand out for the successful family. (This is not the same as the optimally functioning family, discussed in the last chapter. "Optimally functioning family" is a theoretical construct that few families ever completely achieve. One might suppose that the more optimally functioning a family is, the more likely it is to be successful.)

In successful families there is a feeling of empowerment—a feeling that they can make a difference, even when the child has a terminal illness. One of the studies was done with families in which a child had cystic fibrosis. This disease requires that the parents go through a regime of pounding the child on the back in order to clear out the lungs. This is painful for both the child and the parents. Even if they perform this procedure consistently, the child will die eventually. What the researchers found was that the families who followed through were the ones who felt that they could prolong the child's life and make him or her more comfortable; the ones who didn't, felt that there was no use doing anything, because the child was going to die anyway. They felt powerless.

In successful families, the mother's self-esteem is very high. The mother is the one who generally has the responsibility for managing the child's therapy. She is the one family member who is most likely to be involved with the audiologist and the teacher of the deaf. She is the one family member who is most likely to have the responsibility for transmitting what she has learned in school to the home. She is often the one who will have to teach everyone else in the family. If she has high self-esteem, then she values what she knows and is able to enter into a true therapeutic alliance with the teachers. When that happens, the child benefits enormously by the combined efforts of parent and teacher; each has a unique perspective and unique skills. The teacher can guide the course of the therapy. She is an expert on deafness. The mother knows the child as does no one else. She knows what will and what won't work. When she values herself and what she knows, she is willing to share this, to tell the teacher when something won't work for her or for the family; together they can modify educational plans. Parents with low self-esteem do not value what they know and do not share this knowledge; the teacher is thus working in isolation.

A mother with low self-esteem is less likely to direct other family members, which must be done in order to translate the teacher's instructions to the home. A mother who is fearful and insecure is not very effective with her child, her husband, or the child's grandparents. All parents start out fearful and insecure. Parents with high self-esteem quickly shed the fear and treat professionals as equals. Parents with low self-esteem do not value what they know and always feel that others know more than they do. The are often unwilling to direct husbands and grandparents into more appropriate behavior with the deaf child. When this happens, the child suffers.

In a successful family, the burden of deafness is shared, which promotes a feeling that everybody in the family is in this together. In practice, the mother usually is doing the bulk of the work, but if she feels supported by the other family members, she will succeed. The father/husband may never appear at the school, but if he is picking up some of the other family responsibilities and is giving her emotional support, the family will succeed. What has to happen in a successful family is a shift in responsibilities so that the wife/mother, while taking on the added burden of managing the deaf child's home therapies and relating to school, can shed some of her other family responsibilities. Crises have a way of bringing out that which is most noble in all of us. At the time of diagnosis, families invariably come together. This means that each member of the family supports the others. After the immediate crisis is over, however, family members may return to their previous roles. Deafness is a long-term proposition. If the mother is burdened by the deafness and also is expected to do everything she was doing before the crisis without any emotional support, she will feel resentment. She will become a martyr mother. These rarely are successful mothers because they have simmering resentments. Resentful people are invariably saboteurs; they undermine any good result. They tend to want to seek pity from others. They whine and they complain. They create an unpleasant atmosphere in which growth and learning are limited.

Single parent families can be quite successful. Here, the extended family and the community must pitch in and be supportive. If the single parent is getting help from friends and relatives, then he or she can move forward and be successful. In the early stages, all parents feel that they have one hundred ten percent of the responsibility for managing their child's deafness. The reality, as I often tell parents, is that they have only a third. I, as a professional, have a third, and the child has a third. The parents' responsibility is to see that they do one hundred percent of their third, while I'll do one hundred percent of my third, and together we will ensure that the child does one hundred percent of the other third.

The fourth and last characteristic of the successful family is the ability to make philosophical sense of the deafness. Somehow each one of us must come to grips with the question, "Why me?" without a satisfactory answer, we are gripped with bitterness and simmering anger. Rarely are bitter people successful people. Each person's answer to the "Why me?" is unique. You have to find it for yourself. Following are some things I have heard parents of deaf children say:

"Nobody owes me a normal-hearing child, so why *not* me? What is so special about me that I can't have a deaf child."

"This is the hand I was dealt, so I'll play it as well as I can."

"There is some reason I have this child—I can't define God's plan but I know it's there."

A mother with two deaf children and a brain damaged child had this to say:

> "I have no particular talent, no particular anything. I'm a very average type of person. And I've been given three very special kids. Sometimes I talk to God and say, 'Why did you give these kids to me? Why didn't you give them to someone that was different?' and so then I think, "All right, I was given these kids and maybe this is my thing in life. Maybe this is all I'm going to do in life is to get these kids into adulthood, and maybe that is how my salvation will be measured.'"

I recently came across this piece, which I think parents may find very useful. It is reprinted here with the author's permission.

> When you're going to have a baby, it's like planning a wonderful vacation trip to Italy. You get a bunch of guide books and make all your plans. The Coliseum . . . the Michelangelo David . . . the gondolas in Venice. You get a book of handy phrases and learn how to say a few words in Italian. It's all very exciting. Finally, the time comes for your trip. You pack your bags and off you go.
>
> Several hours later, the plane lands. The stewardess comes in and says: "Welcome to Holland."
>
> "Holland?!" you say. "Holland?" I signed up for Italy! All my life I've dreamed of going to Italy!"
>
> "I'm sorry," she says. "There's been a change and we've landed in Holland."
>
> "But I don't know anything about Holland! I never thought of going to Holland. I have no idea what you do in Holland!"
>
> What's important is that they haven't taken you to a terrible ugly place, full of famine, pestilence and disease. It's just—a different place.
>
> So you have to go out and buy a whole new set of guide books . . . you have to learn a whole new language . . . and you'll meet a whole new bunch of people you would never have met otherwise.

Holland. It's slower-paced than Italy, less flashy than Italy . . . but after you've been there for a while, and you've had a chance to catch your breath, you look around and begin to discover that Holland has windmills . . . and Holland has tulips . . . Holland even has Rembrandts.

But everyone you know is busy coming and going from Italy . . . and they're all bragging about what a great time they had there. And for the rest of your life you will say, "Yes, that's where I was supposed to go. That's what I had planned." And the pain of that will never, ever, ever, ever go away. And you must accept that pain—because the loss of that dream is a very, very significant loss.

But . . . if you spend your time mourning the fact that you never got to go to Italy, you may never be available to enjoy the very lovely, very special things about Holland.

Emily Perle Kingsley—*Kids Like These*[3]

Welcome to Holland!

CHAPTER 5

The Audiometric Process

Antonia Brancia Maxon

This chapter is a discussion of the basics of hearing loss including the anatomy of the hearing system, the types of hearing tests that are available, and the clinical results and what they mean. It is important to understand what the tests actually measure and what the results can tell you about what the child can hear.

HEARING SCREENING

Many parents reading this book will have had a child whose hearing loss was identified through newborn hearing screening. For many years it was recommended that infants in neonatal intensive care units (NICU) or those with indicators of risk for hearing loss should have their hearing tested before leaving the hospital. Since the early 1990s universal newborn hearing screening (testing all babies prior to hospital discharge) has been promoted and is continuing to grow. If your child's hearing loss was identified through newborn screening, it is likely that the diagnosis was completely unexpected.

If your child's hearing loss was present at birth, but not identified in the first few months of life, it is very likely you noticed something in his or her behavior that caused you to seek professional help. Your child may have been born with normal hearing and then acquired a hearing loss through illness, trauma, or some other cause of late onset. Sometimes parents are told that their worries are unfounded and that they are being overly concerned. Sometimes they are told that hearing cannot easily be measured in babies. If that did happen, there may have been some delay between the time you noticed a problem and the actual diagnosis of the hearing loss was made.

ANATOMY AND FUNCTION OF THE HEARING MECHANISMS

The ear has three parts: the outer ear, middle ear, and inner ear. As seen in figure 1, the outer ear is made up of the part that is visible (pinna), the ear canal (external auditory meatus), and the eardrum (tympanic membrane). The middle ear cavity is directly behind the eardrum and is typically filled with air. The three small bones (ossicles) that are strung across the cavity

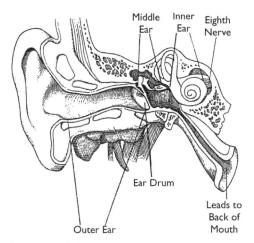

Figure 1.   Anatomy of the ear.

work to direct sound vibration from the eardrum to the inner ear (cochlea). Although not directly part of the hearing mechanism, the Eustachian tube serves an important function for the middle ear. The tube connects the middle ear to the back of the throat and its function is to equalize air pressure in the middle ear cavity so that the pressure is the same as that of the outside air.

Any blockage of the outer or middle ear can cause a conductive hearing loss. Conductive hearing loss may be caused by ear canal blockage by wax or sometimes small objects that a child may put into it. Any such object or material in the ear canal should be removed by a physician. Once the ear canals are cleared hearing levels should return to normal.

The most common childhood medical problem is otitis media with effusion, meaning that the middle ear cavity is filled with fluid and that the fluid may be contaminated with bacteria. When the Eustachian tube is blocked (usually from a cold or allergies) it cannot open and there is negative pressure in the middle ear cavity. If the tube blockage continues, fluid may build up in the middle ear cavity and make it difficult for sound to pass through to the inner ear. Children with otitis media with effusion can have medical treatment (antibiotics) or surgery (inserting tubes in the eardrum) to treat the medical problems and reduce the hearing loss. Conductive hearing loss is not permanent (unless the child has been born with structural damage to the outer or middle ear). It is important to keep in mind that all children are susceptible to outer and middle ear problems regardless of their hearing status.

The third part of the ear, the cochlea, has the critical job of changing the sound vibrations (physical energy) into electrical energy so that the auditory nerve (VIII cranial nerve) can be stimulated and produce neural impulses that are sent to the brain. The cochlea holds all the sensory cells (inner and outer hair cells) that are responsible for generating the electrical impulses. The hair cells have fibers from the VIII nerve in them that carry the neural impulses.

Any damage to cochlear structures or the nerve fibers will result in a hearing loss that is classified as *sensorineural*. There are many possible causes of sensorineural hearing loss that can occur either before birth or at birth (congenital) or during childhood (acquired). The Joint Committee on Infant Hearing (JCIH) has carefully defined the conditions that cause congenital or pediatric acquired hearing loss. The congenital causes include genetic factors, maternal viral infection during pregnancy (cytomegalovirus or CMV is the most common), low birth weight (less than 1500 grams), high bilirubin levels, and certain syndromes. The causes of acquired hearing loss in the pediatric population include viral infection (meningitis is the most common), head trauma, and late-onset genetic factors. Some children have a progressive hearing loss. For these children, the degree of loss increases with age making it critical to monitor hearing levels carefully on a regular basis.

Sensorineural hearing loss is permanent and presently there is no medical treatment that can reduce or eliminate it. All children with sensorineural hearing loss must have a medical evaluation and acquire medical clearance before being fitted with amplification.

Some children are diagnosed with a condition termed *auditory neuropathy*. These children function as if they have sensorineural hearing loss, however they typically do not have cochlear damage or abnormalities. With these children there is always a disparity between what they seem to hear and their audiogram. Therefore, the specific intervention that is recommended for them is dependent upon how well they can use their hearing to acquire communication skills.

AUDIOLOGICAL TERMINOLOGY

Frequency: Frequency is measured in cycles per second (cps), now commonly referred to as Hertz (Hz). The physical sensation of frequency is perceived as pitch. Therefore, the lower the frequency of a sound, the lower in pitch it will sound. The stimuli used in hearing testing are pure tones, that is, they have only one frequency. Humans can hear tones that range from 20 to 20,000 Hz, but routine audiological testing measures a person's responses to a smaller range of specific frequencies.

Intensity: Intensity is the power of the sound that is measured in decibels (dB). The physical sensation of intensity is perceived as loudness. Therefore, the higher the intensity level of a sound, the louder it will seem (e.g., a 90 dB signal is perceived as louder than a 30 dB signal). During audiological testing the audiologist finds the lowest intensity level that a child detects at designated frequencies. The lowest level sound at each frequency is called the threshold for that frequency.

Threshold: The threshold is the lowest intensity level at which a person responds consistently to sounds. In other words, threshold is the softest level of a particular sound that a person can detect. By measuring thresholds at different frequencies the audiologist is able to describe one aspect of hearing which is referred to as the *degree of hearing loss.* More importantly, the audiologist can use these threshold measures to give parents information about the amount of residual hearing a child has, that is, the amount of hearing a child can use to hear environmental and speech sounds.

Air conduction: Hearing is typically tested by having the person use headphones (they may fit over the ears, i.e., circumaural earphones, or into the ears, i.e., insert earphones). When sound is presented via earphones, it travels through the outer, middle, and inner ear on its way to the auditory nerve. During air conduction measurements, the presence of damage or blockage anywhere in the auditory system will result in elevated (poorer than normal) thresholds. That is, regardless of whether a child has a conductive or sensorineural hearing loss, air conduction thresholds will be poorer than normal. Air conduction measurements are used to obtain pure tone thresholds, as well as speech thresholds for each ear.

Bone conduction: Hearing can also be tested by placing a small vibrator on the mastoid bone behind the external ear. When sound is presented via bone conduction it bypasses the outer and middle ear and goes directly to the cochlea, where the sound stimulates the auditory nerve. When hearing is measured by bone conduction, blockage in the outer or middle ear will not affect thresholds, but cochlear damage will. Therefore, a child with a conductive hearing loss will have normal bone conduction thresholds because the cochlea is normal, but a child with sensorineural hearing loss will have elevated bone conduction thresholds. Usually bone conduction is used to measure pure tone thresholds; however, in some situations an audiologist may use it to measure a child's responses to speech.

Sound field: If a child cannot or will not use either type of headphones (over the ear or in the ear), thresholds can be measured by delivering tones and speech sounds through loudspeakers. As the sound is being presented into the air rather than being directed to a particular ear, individual ear thresholds cannot be determined in the sound field. Rather, if the child has different hearing levels in each ear, then only better-ear responses will be obtained. Some audiologists do not attempt to use earphones with infants and toddlers, but you should encourage him or her to use them as soon as possible to obtain good information about residual hearing in each ear.

Audiogram: Figure 2 is an example of an audiogram, a graph that shows a child's thresholds at each frequency tested. By clinical convention intensity (in dB HL) is displayed on the vertical axis with lower intensity at the top and higher intensity at the bottom. Audiograms are used to determine and classify the degree of hearing loss by determining the average

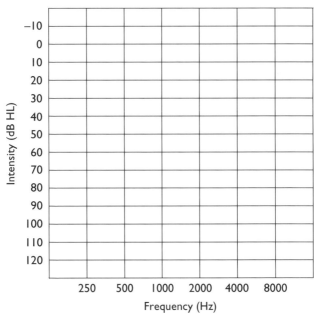

Figure 2.   Clinical audiogram.

threshold dB level. To do that the audiologist will calculate the pure tone average (PTA) which is the average of the child's air conduction thresholds at 500, 1000, and 2000 Hz. Degree of hearing loss classifications (mild, moderate, moderately-severe, severe, profound) are shown on an audiogram in table 1.

Frequency is displayed on the horizontal axis of the audiogram with the lowest frequency on the left and the highest on the right. Air and bone conduction thresholds typically are measured at 250, 500, 1000, 2000, 4000, and 8000 Hz. As children may have different thresholds at different frequencies and there may be significant differences between low and high frequency thresholds, the audiologist will also describe the configuration of the audiogram. By convention, the audiologist will describe the configuration of the child's hearing levels from low to high frequency (left to right). The configuration of the hearing loss will have an effect on the ability to hear the different speech sounds (an explanation of this relationship is presented below).

In order to determine the type of hearing loss (conductive, sensorineural, mixed) the audiologist will compare the air and bone conduction thresholds. On the audiogram air conduction is displayed as circles for the right ear (if in color, the right ear is red) and crosses for the left ear (if in color, the left ear is blue). Bone conduction is generally shown as brackets.

Table 1. Audiometric classification of hearing loss for infants and children.

Normal hearing:	−15 dB HL through 15 dB HL
Minimal hearing loss:	16 dB HL through 25 dB HL
Mild hearing loss:	26 dB HL through 40 dB HL
Moderate hearing loss:	41 dB HL through 55 dB HL
Moderately severe hearing loss:	56 dB HL through 70 dB HL
Severe hearing loss:	71 dB HL through 89 dB HL
Profound hearing loss:	90 dB HL or greater

Figure 3a shows that when a child has a conductive hearing loss, bone conduction thresholds are within normal limits and air conduction thresholds are poorer than normal. A child with sensorineural hearing loss will have an audiogram that displays equally elevated thresholds by air and bone conduction (figure 3b). When a child has a combination of sensorineural and conductive hearing loss there will be a hearing loss by bone conduction as well as air conduction, but air conduction thresholds will be elevated to a greater degree (figure 3c).

DIAGNOSTIC PROCEDURES

Which specific hearing tests the audiologist uses with a child depends on several factors. The major factor is the child's age. The remainder of this chapter presents the types of hearing tests available for children of varying

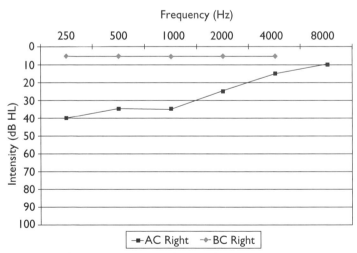

Figure 3a.   Conductive hearing loss in the right ear.

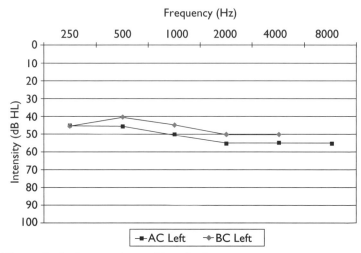

Figure 3b. Left sensorineural hearing loss.

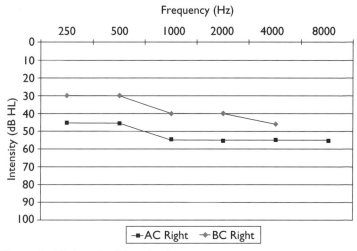

Figure 3c. Right mixed hearing loss.

ages. As some of the tests are appropriate regardless of a child's age, they will be listed in all appropriate sections and include descriptions of any necessary age-appropriate modifications.

Newborn period

Hearing screening procedures may be conducted within the first few weeks of life for the full-term newborn or when the premature infant is medically stable. The specific tests that are used depend primarily on the hospital and in some cases the nursery (regular or neonatal intensive care unit - NICU) in which the child was born. Screening tests are conducted by professionals (nurses, technicians, or designated screeners) who are trained in the processes. Audiologists do not usually carry out the in-hospital screening, but do conduct the follow-up diagnostic procedures for babies who do not pass the newborn screening. The following measurement tools are available for use in hospital-based universal newborn hearing screening programs.

Otoacoustic emissions (OAE) are sounds generated within the cochlea, specifically within the outer hair cells. These hair cells change the mechanical energy of the sound waves into electrical energy after the sound waves enter the cochlea. During this process within the cochlea, the outer hair cells function like mini amplifiers and produce a low-level sound. That sound can travel out of the cochlea, through the middle ear and into the ear canal where it can be measured with a very sensitive microphone.

Otoacoustic emissions are measured by placing a small probe into the ear canal and delivering a click stimulus to the ear. A small microphone that measures the emission is also housed in the probe. As the stimulus and the emission travel through the ear canal and the middle ear, any blockage in the path of the stimulus or the emission itself will interfere. That is, it will reduce the likelihood of an emission occurring or the test's ability to measure it. The most common cause of interference is fluid in the middle ear (middle ear effusion) which will either decrease or completely obliterate the emission.

When the outer hair cells are functioning normally, OAEs are generated. Therefore, the presence of OAEs indicates that hearing levels are close to or within normal limits. It is important to remember that OAEs reflect only the status of the cochlea. If there is a problem in the auditory nerve, OAEs cannot detect it.

The two most common types of OAEs that are measured clinically are transient evoked otoacoustic emissions (TEOAE) and distortion product otoacoustic emissions (DPOAE). Neither type gives specific information about the exact degree, type or configuration of hearing loss, but they do provide information about the status of the cochlea and so are useful in newborn screening.

Another objective measurement that is used in newborn screening is the *auditory brainstem response (ABR)* which occurs when a brief stimulus is delivered through the ear to the auditory nerve (VIII cranial nerve). The ABR is the electrical response of the VIII nerve. The auditory brainstem response is measured by presenting a click stimulus into the ear via an insert earphone. The response of the nerve is measured from electrodes on the infant's scalp.

When the cochlea and the VIII nerve are functioning normally, the ABR will be within normal limits. When there is a hearing loss, presenting the click stimulus results in a less than normal response in the auditory nerve. A modification of the diagnostic ABR, automated auditory brainstem response (AABR), is used in newborn hearing screening because it is quick and easy to conduct.

0-5 months

After a baby is identified through a newborn hearing screening program, a complete diagnostic evaluation is conducted by an audiologist to determine actual hearing status. The initial diagnostic evaluation should include several types of tests to determine the type, degree, and configuration of hearing loss. Otoacoustic emissions can be used for infants in this age group to corroborate the ABR findings.

Diagnostic ABR audiometry is an important component in the pediatric test battery. Unlike the newborn screening, the audiologist uses frequency-specific stimuli and makes both air and bone conduction measures.

Children with auditory neuropathy may have atypical test battery results. They usually have abnormal results on ABR measures, but normal OAE results. In addition it may be difficult to document their actual hearing levels through the behavioral techniques described below.

Behavioral observation audiometry (BOA) is a method that is used to estimate a child's degree and configuration of hearing loss. In this technique, sounds are presented to the infant (either via headphones or the sound field) and his or her unconditioned responses to them are observed and documented. Two audiologists will participate in the testing with the parent and the baby. The parent is usually asked to sit in the test booth with the baby and one of the audiologists will also be present to note the baby's responses. Typical responses that can be consistently observed during a BOA procedure include changes in sucking patterns (during bottle feeding or nursing), eye widening, and changes in activity patterns. When an appointment for this type of evaluation is scheduled, the audiologist may request that for the test the parent tries to ensure that the baby will want to eat and is likely to be drowsy. The second audiologist will carry out the actual testing, presenting the various stimuli.

As the unconditioned responses obtained in a BOA procedure are naturally occurring, they can be elicited only by sounds that are interesting (loud or unusual) enough to capture attention. Therefore, true threshold levels are not obtained, but the audiologist is able to document the infant's *minimal awareness levels (MAL)*. Minimal awareness levels are the lowest intensity levels at which an infant in this age group consistently responds. By documenting MALs, estimates can be made regarding the degree and configuration of the hearing loss.

As it may not be possible to obtain MALs at all of the typical test frequencies listed above, the audiologist may aim for a *target audiogram*. When doing this, the audiologist attempts to measure MALs at a low (250 or 500 Hz), mid (1000 Hz), and high (4000 Hz) frequency sound. In this way the audiologist can predict the configuration of the hearing loss by interpolating from the measured response levels to those that were not measured. This information can be used to predict how much access the baby has to all of the speech sounds.

Although this prediction can be made, it is also important to observe how the child actually responds to speech at different intensity levels. Therefore, the audiologist will first measure the lowest intensity level at which speech is just detected, that is obtain a *speech awareness threshold (SAT)*. In doing this, the audiologist may babble ("ma, ma, ma"), call the child's name, or make unusual sounds (lip trilling). It is expected that the MALs and SAT will be within about 10 dB of each other with the SAT being better (at a lower intensity level). That is because babies prefer speech to tones and are able to respond at lower levels.

6-24 months

By the time an infant reaches six months of age, he or she is able to localize the source of a sound and can learn to give a consistent response (head turning) during hearing testing. The audiological technique that is most commonly used for infants in this age group is *visual reinforcement audiometry (VRA)*, that is, one in which an infant's appropriate response to a tone or speech is reinforced with a visual stimulus. (Usually two audiologists are used in this procedure, one who sits in the booth and one who presents the stimuli.) A parent usually sits in the booth with the child and at the start of the test the audiologist will train the baby to turn in the direction of a sound source (loudspeaker, insert earphone, bone conduction vibrator) by presenting a sound (pulsed or warbled tone) and an animated toy simultaneously. Once the child has realized that the toy will move or light up whenever a sound occurs, the audiologist will then move to actual testing. In this phase, a sound is presented, the audiologist waits for the baby to look in the direction of the sound and then the toy is presented as a reinforcer for the response. When using a VRA technique, consistent, repeatable responses can be obtained down to threshold levels. Therefore, depending on the baby's continued interest in the reinforcers, complete or target audiograms can readily be obtained.

As indicated above *threshold* is the lowest intensity level at which a consistent response to sound is measured. Using VRA, threshold responses can be measured and the type, degree, and configuration of the audiogram can be described. The baby's responses to speech can also be determined, obtaining an SAT using a visual reinforcement procedure. In addition, when the child is a toddler his or her ability to respond appropriately to speech presented at a comfortable listening level also can be found. In this procedure, the audiologist presents speech (requests, questions) at a level 30-40 dB about the SAT and the toddler will respond by pointing to familiar objects, people, body parts, etc. In some cases, the audiologist may use specific speech sounds (the Ling six-sound test). In this test, the child's reaction to a variety of speech sounds ("ah", "ee" ,"oo", "s", "sh", "m") is observed.

25-60 months

As toddlers approach three years of age they are more likely to be tested using a *conditioned play audiometry (CPA)* technique. In this method, the child is trained to carry out a motor activity (throwing a ball in a bucket, putting a block in a box) in response to tones to obtain a complete threshold level audiogram. For CPA, one or two audiologists may be involved, but as with the other procedures, a parent is usually in the test booth with the child. If no audiologist is in the test booth, the parent will help condition the child to carry out the motor task (e.g., handing him or her the ball to throw). Air and bone conduction measures can readily be carried out using this procedure.

Speech audiometry measures conducted at this time may be more formal. As older children may have better vocabulary, a speech reception threshold (SRT) can be measured. Speech reception thresholds are determined by presenting spondee words (familiar two-syllable words with equal stress on each syllable, e.g., "hotdog") and having the child point to toys or pictures that represent the spondees (older children may be able to repeat the words). It is important for you to help the audiologist know whether the child actually knows the test words being used. If the child does not know a particular word (e.g., "cowboy"), it should not be included as a test item, because this is a test of hearing level, not of language level. Like the SAT, the SRT should be similar in intensity level to the tone thresholds. Specifically, the SRT and PTA should be within 10 dB of each other.

A child's ability to hear the various sounds of comfortable level speech may be measured by *speech recognition testing*. A speech recognition test consists of measurements that can be carried out using familiar *monosyllabic* words. These words should be within the child's receptive vocabulary (i.e., the child needs to know the particular word). Again, if a child does not know a particular word being used, it should not be calculated into the score obtained. Children with a three-year-old vocabulary level can be tested by using a test like the Word Intelligibility by Picture Identification (WIPI) or the Northwestern University Children's Hearing Perception Test (NU-CHIPS). In these procedures, the audiologist presents words that are represented by pictures and the child points to the correct picture (selecting one out of six or four on a page). These picture- pointing tests are usually scored as whole word correct and a percent correct score is obtained.

Speech recognition scores are related to the configuration of the audiogram. Specifically, a high frequency hearing loss will result in difficulty hearing some of the voiceless consonants like "s" and "f." Speech recognition testing provides invaluable information about the child's use of hearing for access to speech. Such testing can be used to gauge auditory skill development and to plan listening therapy. Regardless of the actual test that is used (it may be different from those described above) it is important for the audiologist to give parents specific information about what their child is hearing at comfortable listening levels.

Older children

Conventional audiometry techniques (e.g., a child raises his or her hand as a response to hearing a sound) may be used when a child is at least five-years old developmentally. Air and bone conduction threshold can be obtained to acquire a complete audiogram. For children who can use conventional methods, SRTs and speech recognition scores may be obtained either with picture pointing or by having the child repeat the word (talk back), depending on the clarity of the child's speech. If the audiologist has difficulty understanding the child's speech, picture pointing is the method of choice. In speech recognition testing, the results can be scored as percent of whole words correct, however, to truly determine how much access the child has to different speech sounds, the audiologist should use a phoneme scoring technique.

Different scoring techniques provide very different levels of information. Take the example of the stimulus word "cat" to which the child replies "pat." Whole word scoring would give the child no credit or 0% correct. If phoneme scoring is used, the child would receive credit for hearing the vowel ("ah") and the final consonant ("t") correctly. Therefore, phoneme scoring provides a more complete understanding of what aspects of the speech signal the child hears or does not hear.

IMMITTANCE MEASURES

As mentioned above, middle ear disease is very common in early childhood regardless of hearing status. Therefore, it is important to assess the status of the middle ear during an audiological evaluation. In order to do so, the audiologist uses a battery of tests typically referred to as *immittance measures*.

Tympanometry is used to determine if there is an abnormal condition like a perforated eardrum, fluid, or negative pressure in the middle ear cavity. Tympanometry is carried out by placing a small probe in the ear canal so a pure tone (usually low frequency) can be introduced while varying the ear pressure. It is not necessary for the child to hear the tone. Rather, it is used as a means of determining stiffness of the middle ear system by measuring how much of the tone is passed on or reflected by the eardrum.

To measure reflected sound, the probe contains a small microphone. When the air pressure on either side of the tympanic membrane is equal then the eardrum is very compliant and little sound is reflected. If the air pressure in the middle ear cavity is normal, then a normal tympanogram is obtained. Tympanometry provides information about middle ear status and not hearing status, so a normal tympanogram can be obtained whether a child has normal hearing or has a sensorineural hearing loss.

Abnormal tympanograms are obtained when there are abnormal conditions in the middle ear. The following are examples of the type of tympanograms that are associated with the two most common abnormal pediatric middle ear conditions. Children who have Eustachian tube dysfunction, but have no fluid in the middle ear cavity typically have negative pressure in the middle ear. The resulting tympanogram will show normal compliance of the eardrum, but a negative air pressure peak ($\geq$ –100mm/H2O). When a child has middle ear effusion (fluid in the middle ear cavity), the eardrum will be very stiff and show little or no movement with changes in air pressure. This *flat* tympanogram occurs because the maximum amount of the probe tone is being reflected back toward the probe microphone.

Another test in the middle ear measurement battery is determining the *stapedial reflex thresholds*. When loud sounds (greater than 70 dB) are introduced into a normally functioning ear, one of the middle ear muscles (stapedius) contracts very rapidly and stiffens the whole middle ear system. (The biological function of this reflex is to protect the ear from loud sounds.) In stapedial reflex testing a loud tone is sent through the tympanometry probe to attempt to stimulate the reflex. The stiffness of the eardrum is then measured in the brief period immediately after the loud tone is sent through the probe, by determining the amount of the probe tone that is reflected back to the probe microphone. As in tympanometry, the stiffer the middle ear system, the more sound is reflected. Therefore, stapedius muscle contraction can be indirectly measured by determining if the eardrum is stiffer than normal in the presence of loud sounds.

Sensorineural hearing loss of great enough degree will reduce or eliminate stapedius muscle contraction (the sound does not have enough intensity in the damaged cochlea to be loud). Conductive hearing loss will also interfere with measurement of stapedial reflexes. With conductive hearing loss, the middle ear system is already stiff (e.g., from fluid in the middle ear) and therefore a change in the system will not be observable even if the stapedius contracts.

DISCUSSION

Audiological assessment is an important part of programming for a child with hearing loss. Pure tone audiograms should be considered a description of what a child hears, specifically his or her residual hearing. Suprathreshold speech recognition scores give parents and service providers information about a child's potential for using the acoustic components of the speech signal.

Parents should always feel that they have a complete understanding of the tests that the audiologist has conducted, as well as the specific results obtained at each evaluation. If at any time a parent feels that something is not clear, the audiologist should take the time to explain it. It is not unusual to need or want to hear explanations and clarifications multiple times. As parents acquire more knowledge about hearing and audiological techniques, they will want more in-depth discussions with the audiologist. As a child gets older, more detailed and specific information can be obtained and should be made available to parents.

It is particularly important that parents be familiar with the specific benefit that the child receives from his or her amplification or other sensory device. The next chapter contains information about the available devices, how they are selected, and how they are used and evaluated.

CHAPTER 6

Amplification and Other Sensory Devices

Antonia Brancia Maxon

PURPOSE OF SENSORY DEVICES

After a child is diagnosed with sensorineural hearing loss, an audiologist works with the family to find the most appropriate sensory device(s). These devices include hearing aids, FM systems and cochlear implants. The primary purpose of any sensory device is to help the child hear to provide maximal access to the speech signal to afford the child the best possible opportunity to acquire and use spoken language for communication.

MAXIMIZING RESIDUAL HEARING AND ACCESSING THE SPEECH SIGNAL

The primary purpose of sensory devices is to provide maximal exposure to the speech spectrum. Speech covers a wide range of frequencies from low to high. Most vowel sounds are in the low to mid-frequency range while much of the acoustic energy of consonant sounds is in the mid-to-high frequency range. The more of that frequency range (100-10,000 Hz) the sensory device can deliver, the easier it is for an infant or young child to discriminate among the speech sounds. In order to do this, a child must receive the speech signal at a loudness level that is greater than just detectable. With an appropriate dynamic range (softest to loudest sounds heard) children can hear and discriminate among the loudest sounds (typically vowels) as well as the softest sounds (consonants like /s/). Tables 1a and 1b show how the speech signal varies across frequency and intensity. Young children who are developing speech must be able to hear the speech of others, as well as their own speech. In this way, children develop an auditory feedback loop that allows them to match what they are producing to what others are saying.

Table 1a.   Frequency characteristics of English consonants.

Consonant	Frequency Bands (Hz) 1	2 3	4
r (red)	600-800	1000-1500	1800-2400
l (let)	250-400		2000-3000
sh (shot)			1500-2000	4500-5000
ng (wing)	250-400	1000-1500	2000-3000
ch (chat)		1500-2000		4000-5000
n (no)	250-300	1000-1500	2000-3000
m (me)	250-300	1000-1500	2500-3500
th (that)	250-350			4500-6000
t (tap)			2500-3500
h (hat)		1500-2000
k (kit)			2000-2500
j (jot)	200-300		2000-3000
f (for)				4000-5000
g (get)	200-300	1500-2500
s (sit)				5000-6000
z (zip)	200-300			4000-5000
v (vat)	300-400			3500-4500
p (pat)		1500-2000
d (dot)	300-400		2500-3000
b (bat)	300-400		2000-2500
th (thin)				~6000

Table 1b. Frequency characteristics of English vowels spoken by women.

	ee b<u>ee</u>t	I b<u>i</u>t	eh b<u>e</u>t	ae b<u>a</u>t	ah sp<u>a</u>	aw s<u>a</u>w	U b<u>oo</u>k	oo b<u>oo</u>t	uh b<u>u</u>t
F0	235	232	223	210	212	216	232	231	221
F1	310	430	610	860	850	590	470	370	760
F2	2790	2480	2330	2050	1220	920	1160	950	1400
F3	3310	3070	2990	2850	2810	2710	2680	2670	2780

Usable access to sound allows children to hear and produce speech and then deduce the rules of language that are dependent on these sounds. For example, /s/ is an important grammatical marker in spoken English. It is used to indicate plural ("one hat" vs. "two hats"), possession ("a cat" vs. "a cat's toy"), and noun-verb agreement ("the girl sits" vs. "the girls sit"). Table 1 shows that /s/ is a high frequency sound. When a sensory device provides auditory access to /s/ in typical listening situations, children have the potential of deducing grammatical rules like those given above. When the device does not amplify and deliver that sound, children have to be taught language rules and have to depend on other cues to "fill in" what is not heard.

HEARING AIDS

Any device that is designed to amplify sound will take a signal (speech and environmental) and increase it in intensity or loudness. Children with hearing loss can benefit from receiving amplified speech and environmental sounds. They can use that amplified sound to develop speech perception, speech production, and spoken/auditory language.

All hearing aids are made up of similar basic components: a microphone, amplifier, transducer, and power supply. Sounds (acoustic signals) are picked up by the hearing aid microphone and changed to electrical energy. The electrical signal is then amplified and modified after which it is delivered to the transducer. The transducer turns the electrical signal back into acoustic energy and delivers it to the child's ears.

Hearing aids are selected by the electroacoustic characteristics (frequency response, gain, output) that suit the child's hearing loss. By setting these features the most appropriate amplified signal can be delivered to each child. Gain is the amount of amplification a hearing aid can provide. Audiologists generally define gain by describing the average amount of amplification (in dB) of a hearing aid. The greater the degree of hearing loss a child has, the more gain he or she will need. As discussed in the previous chapter, the degree of hearing loss may not be the same across frequencies, therefore the audiologist chooses the hearing aid that has an appropriate amount of amplification at all frequencies. If a child has poorer hearing in the high frequencies the *frequency response* has to reflect that and provide more gain in that region. Although children with hearing loss need sounds to be presented at an increased loudness level, they do not want sound to be uncomfortably loud. Therefore, the maximum amount of sound that a hearing aid will deliver is determined by the *output*.

In addition, custom-made earmolds (fabricated from impressions taken of the child's outer ear and ear canal) deliver the amplified signal from the hearing aid to the child's ears. It is crucial that earmolds fit very snugly in the child's outer ear. With infants and young children that may mean that the audiologist must take impressions for new earmolds once or twice each month to accommodate the changes in growing ears. If earmolds do not fit properly the amplified sound will leak out and it will be picked up again by the microphone.

Then the hearing aid will amplify this signal again causing a high pitched whistle (acoustic feedback). This sound is unpleasant and interferes with what the child hears.

For older children and adults earmolds may be modified to change the frequency characteristics of the sound after it has been amplified by the hearing aid and before it is delivered to the child. If the child has relatively good hearing in the low frequencies a vent (a small opening) can be made to the outside of the earmold so that low frequency amplification is reduced. The length of the earmold canal can also be adjusted. A short canal length will reduce the low frequency amplification while increasing that in the high frequency region. The high frequencies can also be increased by flaring the opening of the sound bore (a megaphone shape). Actual benefit of these earmold modifications is dependent on the size and shape of a child's ear. Therefore, to be certain that the desired acoustic effects have been achieved, the audiologist should test the child with the modified earmolds.

As most children with impaired hearing have a hearing loss in both ears they will need two (binaural) hearing aids. Using two hearing aids allows children to acquire some of the advantages of using two ears. Specifically, they can learn to localize a sound— determine where a sound is coming from—and develop auditory spatial perception. When using binaural hearing aids, children may also hear speech better in noisy listening environments. Therefore, binaural amplification is generally the most appropriate fitting for children.

There are different types of hearing aids, but some are not appropriate for infants, toddlers, and young children. Only those that are appropriate for the pediatric population will be described and discussed.

Behind-the-Ear (BTE) hearing aids have all of the components described previously housed in a relatively small case that fits behind the pinna. (The earmold attaches to the hearing aid by a length of clear tubing.) These hearing aids usually have a lot of electroacoustic flexibility so that the settings can continue to be modified as the audiologist acquires more specific information about the child's hearing. A potential problem with BTE hearing aids is the close positioning of the microphone to the transducer. With a loosely fitting earmold, acoustic feedback is likely to occur due to the proximity of those two components. As indicated above, this problem can be avoided by ensuring that the earmolds fit tightly.

Recent technology allows audiologists a variety of options for finding the most appropriate device for a child. Behind-the-ear options that may be considered for the pediatric population are presented in this section.

Programmable hearing aids typically use analogue processing. That is, the signal is processed in the manner described above. The difference between traditional and programmable hearing aids is that electroacoustic characteristics are applied through computer programming in the latter, rather than by hand (using a small screwdriver). Programming the hearing aid often gives the audiologist the ability to set the hearing aid more precisely.

Digital hearing aids depend on technology that applies the electroacoustic characteristics after the acoustic signal has been converted from analogue to digital. Because these hearing aids use a more advanced technology, they have the potential to provide a very finely tuned sound to the child's ear. The difficulty in fitting digital hearing aids to young children is that they cannot participate in the type of task (repeating words) that typically allows for such precise settings.

Some digital and analogue hearing aids have the potential to keep two or more different sets of electroacoustic characteristics (called programs) in the device at the same time. This type of hearing aid is often chosen if the child has to function in a variety of different listening conditions on a regular basis. The family and audiologist can work together to develop separate programs that may be appropriate for listening in noise and listening in quiet. They may also choose to develop programs that can be used with other assistive devices (an FM system) or technology (the telephone).

Frequency transposition hearing aids are used for children who have poor high frequency hearing. Most hearing aids (analogue and digital) have limited reproduction of sound above 4000 Hz. Table 1 shows that there is important speech information above that frequency (particularly /s/). Therefore, children with poorer high frequency hearing will have almost no access to some important speech cues. Frequency transposition takes high frequency sounds and reproduces them in a lower frequency region, making them audible to the child without interfering with low frequency hearing. These hearing aids are programmable, allowing the audiologist to select carefully and transpose only the necessary frequency regions for a particular child.

Bone conduction hearing aids are recommended for children who cannot accommodate an earmold due to outer ear malformations or chronic drainage. An amplified signal is delivered directly to the inner ear through a hearing aid that uses a bone vibrator as a transducer.

HEARING AID SELECTION AND FITTING

The selection and fitting of hearing aids should begin immediately after a child's hearing loss has been diagnosed, even if the child is very young. An audiologist does not need exhaustive audiological information to help you in deciding on the most appropriate hearing aids for your child. An audiologist will use the target audiogram (and any other information that was obtained) and conduct other measures (described below) to help in the decision-making process. Table 2 shows the basic audiological data a pediatric audiologist can use to select and fit amplification.

A pediatric audiologist will want to use a prescriptive approach to the hearing aid fitting. This method uses audiological information and measurements of the physical characteristics of a child's ear to determine the best electroacoustic characteristics for that child. Presently, many prescriptive fitting procedures are available for adults, but the only one designed specifically for infants and children is the Desired Sensation Level (DSL) developed by Seewald et al. (1996). This method, which makes adjustments for pediatric ears, uses real ear measurements to determine the target gain and output settings without requiring much audiometric data.

Table 2. Basic audiological data needed to select and fit amplification for a young child.

1. Hearing sensitivity
    a. ABR click + low frequency tones, or
    b. Frequency-specific ABR, or
    c. Target audiogram, and
    d. Individual ear measures (insert earphones or localization)

2. Middle ear status
    a. tympanometry—high frequency probe tone when necessary
    b. bone conduction ABR, or
    c. bone conduction target audiogram

3. Tolerance
    a. stapedial reflexes—high frequency probe tone when necessary

The DSL goal is to provide optimal gain across the maximum frequency range. The purpose is to provide optimal access to the speech signal in a variety of listening conditions. This ensures that an infant or young child who is developing language has access to the speech of others, as well as to his or her own speech.

It is important to note that the hearing aid fitting and validation is an ongoing procedure. The pediatric audiologist will want to select a flexible hearing aid so that changes can be made in electroacoustic settings as more audiological data become available. Parents, early intervention professionals, and the pediatric audiologist all work together in refining the hearing aid fitting. Parents are often called upon to provide information about their child's reactions to environmental and speech sounds, as well as communication strategies and behaviors.

FM SYSTEMS

Even when a child has the most appropriately fit hearing aids there will be listening situations in which it is very difficult to understand speech. The environmental conditions that cause the greatest difficulties are increased background noise levels, distance from the sound source, highly reverberant rooms, and any combination of these three. These conditions set up poor speech-to-noise ratios (S/N), that is the intensity level of the speech relative to the background noise. Negative S/Ns make very difficult listening conditions. In general, any time that a child is in increased noise and/or at a distance from the talker his or her ability to understand the speech will be negatively affected. Difficult listening situations that may arise at home and preschool or in regular school situations and where an FM system would be beneficial are shown in table 3.

There are a number of different models of FM systems, personal and sound field types. For all types, the talker uses a wireless microphone and transmitter. The microphone picks up the talker's speech, converts it to electrical energy and superimposes it onto a carrier wave (FM radio wave) that is transmitted through the air to a receiver. For the personal FM systems, the listener wears a receiver (coupled to an amplification system) that has environmental microphones (to pick up environmental sounds and the child's own speech) mounted on it. For the sound field type, the receiver is coupled to an amplified loudspeaker and the child uses his or her own personal sensory device in conjunction with it. In either type, the child hears what the talker is saying at a consistent intensity level. Because the talker is wearing the microphone close to the mouth, the problems of distance from the talker are overcome. In addition, the signal from the remote microphone is set louder than the signal from the child's unit, thus creating a positive signal-to-noise ratio and overcoming the problem of listening in noise.

Table 3. Conditions in which an FM systems is beneficial

Condition	Example	Age
Distance from talker	food preparation	Infant
	crawling/cruising	Infant/toddler
	playground	older child
	teacher talking	school-age child
Background Noise	party/restaurant	all ages
	day care/preschool	infant-five years
	cafeteria	school-age child
Distance and Noise	lecture hall	school-age child
	house of worship	all ages

Personal FM systems include traditional (receiver and environmental microphones worn on a body-worn unit), BTE (receiver and environmental microphones housed in a device that fits behind the ear), and wireless boots that attach to the child's personal BTE hearing aids. Children who use cochlear implants may use an *insert FM receiver* that couples to the speech processor.

Children with hearing aids and cochlear implants may use a sound field FM system in conjunction with their personal devices. In the *traditional sound field system*, loud-speakers are mounted on the walls (typically in a classroom) and the child sits close to the speakers. With a *personal sound field*, a single small portable loud-speaker is placed close to the child (approximately 18" away).

FM systems should be selected and fitted the same way that hearing aids are. These listening systems should be recommended by the audiologist as soon as difficult listening conditions are determined.

COCHLEAR IMPLANTS

Some children are unable to benefit from any type of traditional amplification (either hearing aids or personal FM system). For these children the sensory device of choice is likely to be a cochlear implant. The present criteria for cochlear implant candidacy are:

1. bilateral severe to profound sensorineural hearing loss,
2. age 12 months or older,
3. little or no useful benefit from traditional hearing aids—for older children that is measured as less than 20% best aided word score, and

4. no medical contraindications (that is, the child can safely undergo surgery, including anesthesia.

Audiologists can help parents determine if their child is an implant candidate by considering other factors. Those indicators include:

1. the child shows limited or no detection of amplified speech,
2. the child has little or no response to amplified speech including alerting (near or far),
3. the child has poor responses to high frequency speech sounds with very limited responses to low frequencies,
4. interactive responses in intervention or educational setting and at home are limited, and
5. the child has limited responses to environmental and common sounds (e.g., knocking on the door).

A cochlear implant electrically stimulates the auditory nerve and includes two types of components, internal and external.

The internal components include a magnet, a receiver, and an electrode array. The receiver and magnet package is surgically placed in the skull behind the pinna and the electrode is threaded into the cochlea. The specific number of electrodes and the way they are stimulated varies by manufacturer and device.

The external components include a microphone, transmitter, and magnet on the headpiece, as well as a speech processor (body-worn or BTE). The body-worn speech processor is connected to the headpiece by a wire. There are also models in which the speech processor and head set are incorporated into a single behind-the-ear unit. In both types, the microphone picks up the acoustic signal and changes it to electrical energy that is delivered to the speech processor. There the signal is electrically coded (using a speech processing strategy) and then delivered to the transmitter which sends the signal to the internal receiver. The electrodes are then stimulated and in turn, stimulate the VIII cranial nerve.

The audiologist works with the child, family, and aural rehabilitation provider to determine the speech processing strategy that will provide optimal speech understanding. As cochlear implants do not deliver acoustic energy to the ear, the child's electrical thresholds and comfort levels must be determined.

This is not carried out with an audiometer in a sound proof booth; rather the audiologist makes these measurements (mapping) through a specially programmed computer.

MAINTAINING AND MONITORING AMPLIFICATION AND SENSORY DEVICES

Once a hearing aid or FM system is selected and fitted, or a cochlear implant is mapped, it is important to monitor the device's function. Daily checking and troubleshooting of the device ensures that any malfunction is quickly found and repaired. Table 4 lists the equipment and supplies needed for monitoring. With hearing aids and FM systems, parents can listen to the device through a listening tube or stethoscope. Any change in quality or intensity of the sound should be immediately addressed. By working with the child's audiologist parents will become familiar with the devices, how they should sound, and how to do simple repairs (such as changing cords or eliminating moisture). As cochlear implants do not deliver an acoustic signal,

Table 4. Monitoring and troubleshooting sensory devices

Equipment for hearing aids and FM systems
    battery tester
    listening tube/stethoscope/earmold
    earmold cleaner
    air blower
    wax remover
    dry pouch

Equipment for cochlear implants
    signal checker
    listening earphones
    external microphone

Backup supplies for hearing aids and FM systems
    batteries
    cords
    transducers
    antennae

Backup supplies for cochlear implants
    batteries
    cords

parents cannot listen to them. Therefore, they have to depend on checking with the equipment listed.

Even when families and audiologists have carefully selected and fitted the appropriate sensory devices, some practical problems can arise during daily activities. Those problems and possible solutions are presented in table 5.

ASSISTIVE DEVICES

Assistive devices are used in conjunction with a hearing aid, FM system, or cochlear implant so that access to all types of sounds can be achieved. Many types of devices are commercially available and some should be considered for the pediatric population.

Table 5. Issues with sensory devices that may arise daily.

Problem	Solutions
Difficulty keeping BTE unit on the ear	Huggies, Strap holder, Microphone lock
Child removes batteries	Battery door lock
Earmolds pulled off H.A.	Replace mold, replace tubing
Changing volume on H.A.	Volume control cover
Changing volume on C.I.	Locking controls
Blinking, flinching to loud sounds	Decrease H.A. output or gain; Decrease C.I. comfort levels
Facial "twitching" with C.I.	Decrease current levels
Pulling out H.A. earmolds	Remake or refit earmolds; Remake with hypoallergenic material
Acoustic feedback	Remake loose earmolds; Medical treatment for wax or middle ear fluid
Inflammation at C.I. magnet	Decrease magnet strength
Not responding to high pitches	Change H.A. settings; Try frequency transposition H.A.; Change C.I. map
Blinking, startling low frequencies	Change frequency response of H.A.; Change C.I. map

Alerting devices allow children to know that the doorbell or telephone is ringing. Through these devices they become more aware of sounds in their daily environments and develop important sound-object associations.

Direct audio input is a hard-wired connection from an auditory device (television, radio, audio cassette, CD player, computer) to a hearing aid, FM system, or cochlear implant. Such a connection provides a positive signal-to-noise ratio and allows the child to hear entertaining and educational audio material.

Telephone amplifiers or wired input allow the child to hear on the telephone. Through these devices, a young child learns to interact with extended family members and gains more communication experience.

DISCUSSION

Sensory devices for children with hearing loss are critical for listening, speech and language learning. By working closely with a pediatric audiologist, parents can determine which device will provide the best auditory input for their child. As this process is ongoing and takes place in the home as well as in the audiological clinic, it is important that the family and audiologist have a positive working relationship. Some indicators that help in selecting an audiologist are found in table 6. In general, a pediatric audiologist must be able to respond immediately to parents' and children's needs. This includes quickly providing amplification and making appropriate recommendations.

Table 6. Selecting a pediatric audiologist

1. The audiologist schedules an appointment a short time after parent contact;
2. The audiologist specializes in working with infants and young children;
3. The audiologist recommends hearing aids for the child in a timely manner;
4. The audiologist makes earmold impressions, dispenses hearing aids and provides hearing aids on a trial basis;
5. The audiologist provides loaner hearing aids and can have hearing aids repaired in a timely manner;
6. The audiologist has worked with early intervention systems and is familiar with IFSP development and procedures for acquiring sensory devices;
7. The audiologist discusses the results of audiological evaluations with the family and provides a comprehensive written report, with a copy of the audiogram in a timely manner.

CHAPTER 7

Educational Choices

I approach writing this chapter with some trepidation because no matter what I say, somebody will be offended. The issue of methodology is a swamp and it's very hard for professionals and parents to pick their way through the morass and land on solid ground. There is little hard research evidence that one can depend on in order to make informed decisions, although there are loads of opinions floating around and many people who would be more than willing to tell you how to raise your deaf child and which educational method to use. There is a long history of the controversy.[4]

There are two broad approaches to educating deaf persons: one advocates some form of sign language or manual-assisted system, and the other, known as oralism, advocates the use of lipreading (speechreading) and the development of the child's residual auditory capacity. Oralism discourages, sometimes actively, the use of any form of manual assistance. The underlying philosophy of the oralist is to make the hearing-impaired child as much like a normal hearing person as possible; in short, to minimize deafness as a handicap.

The manual school is very concerned about the self-esteem of the deaf child and wants to have a well-adjusted deaf child. (The oral school is also concerned about self-esteem, but does not talk about it very much.) The manual school does not see deafness as a handicap necessarily, but as a cultural difference that needs to be respected. The emphasis in all the manual approaches is on communication; oralists will talk more about normalcy. Within each camp, there are divergences as well. The oralists split among those who would be very visual and specifically teach the child to lipread, as opposed to the auralists (whose method is sometimes referred to as unisensory or auditory/verbal) who believe that the deaf child should be approached as a limited-hearing child. The auralist tries to train the residual hearing, while the oralist tries to compensate for the reduced acuity by training the intact senses, mainly vision. Oralists may do a great deal of auditory training, but they still appeal to the deaf child's visual sense in any communication. An oralist will always stand in front of the child when talking, with a clear light on his or her face; an auralist may be alongside the child and may even cover the speaker's face Auralists also limit any exposure the child might have to other deaf children. Everything is to be "normal."

The manual school is also divided. There are those educators who believe that the child should be taught with a manually coded English system, as opposed to those who believe the child should be educated using American Sign Language (ASL). ASL is a sign language developed by deaf people themselves. The grammatical structure of ASL is unique because it is visually based, and therefore bares no relation to the syntax of oral or written English. In the 1960s, when educators decided to introduce manual communication into the mainstream of education of the deaf, they decided to recast ASL into a manually coded English system. They took the root forms of ASL and added signs to make ASL equivalent to English. For example, ASL has no sign for prefixes or suffixes, so they were added. They also changed the syntax of ASL so that it corresponded with oral English.

Manually coded English permitted the development of total communication (TC), which tries to bridge the gap between oralism and ASL. In the total communication approach, the children wear hearing aids and are encouraged to lipread; the teachers speak and at the same time use some form of manually coded English (there are six systems), which corresponds word-for-word with spoken English, at least in theory.

The deaf community and some educators of the deaf frown on the bastardization of ASL into a manually coded English system. Its proponents feel that ASL is the natural language and, therefore, easy and natural for the deaf child to learn. They feel that it is easier to learn a new language when you already know one language; they think that the child should be taught ASL first and then acquire English as a second language (this is often referred to as the bi-lingual/bi-cultural approach). In order to teach ASL, you do not speak (spoken English and ASL are two different languages). This group, which is composed of many deaf adults and some educators, does not want to make deaf children like hearing children. They are indifferent to hearing aids and to emphasizing speech. They are very proud of being deaf and see deafness as a cultural difference rather than as a disability. They encourage the children to be proud of being deaf. Speech is at best an optional activity.

There is a fifth school of thought that uses a manual code to enhance lipreading; it is known as cued speech. All other manual systems give the child information about the words being used; cued speech is a system that provides information about the phonemes (sounds) of spoken English. Lipreading English is very difficult because there are a number of phonemes that look alike on the lips but sound different because some are voiced and some are voiceless. For example, "p" and "b" are cognate pairs; the difference between them is that "p" is voiceless and is produced with the vocal folds open, while "b" is voiced and produced with the vocal folds closed. You cannot see the difference but you can hear it. If you are deaf, you cannot differentiate one from the other, so that "pail" looks identical to "bail." You need the sentence context in order to tell them apart. In cued speech, there are different hand signals for the "p" and the "b," enabling you to lipread the words; it is a visual assist to an oral system. The system is useless without spoken words.

These, then are the five most common educational methodologies being used today; oralism, auralism, ASL, total communication, and cued speech. A recent study[5] that looked at the various methodologies concluded that there is no one satisfactory method for educating all deaf children. In the main, the academic achievements, oral and written English proficiency, and speech ability of most deaf children are poor, although there are large numbers of children who do surprisingly well in their academic achievements. Despite the incredibly hard work of teachers of the deaf, there are no responsible educators of the deaf who are entirely happy with the attainments of students who graduate from programs for the deaf. In 1988, the Commission on Education of the Deaf opened its report with the following statement:

> The present status of education for persons who are deaf in the United States is unsatisfactory. Unacceptably so, this is the primary and inescapable conclusion of the Commission on Education of the Deaf.

In the United States, the oldest established school for the deaf is the American School for the Deaf in Hartford, Connecticut, founded in 1817. Its first principal was Thomas Hopkins Gallaudet, who was sent to

Europe specifically to study methods of educating the deaf. He first went to England where an oralist philosophy was in vogue, but he apparently was not treated well at the school, where methods were not openly shared with outsiders. He went on to France and studied at a school founded by the Abbé Dè Lépee. The story goes that the good Abbé discovered among his parishioners deaf sisters who communicated beautifully by use of sign language. He became fascinated with their ability to communicate, and he set about learning their sign system. He also canvassed the city of Paris and found a number of deaf children in the city and was able to convince the authorities to provide funds for a school for the deaf. This was the first example of the government taking responsibility for educating children with special needs. Up to that time, schools were either private or parochial. The Abbé's school used sign language exclusively, and while he believed it was possible to teach deaf children to speak, he placed little emphasis on it. He devoted a great deal of time and effort toward codifying the sign system he was developing.

The Abbé's system, modified by the Americans, became the basis for ASL, which was brought here by Gallaudet. The American School flourished and became the primary training center for teachers of the deaf in the United States. As other states established schools, they sent prospective teachers to the American School to study.

In 1867, the first oral school for the deaf was established in Massachusetts—Clarke School for the Deaf. Thus was born the split in education of the deaf in the United States. During the latter part of the nineteenth century, the split between oral and manual education in the U.S. became personified in a battle between two men: Alexander Graham Bell, an oralist, and Edward Miner Gallaudet, son of Thomas Hopkins

Gallaudet and his deaf wife, who believed strongly that sign language was a necessary component of education for deaf children. Unlike his father, he put more emphasis on teaching speech and developed the "simultaneous method," which involved talking and using ASL, a forerunner of *total communication* (TC).

Bell, on the other hand, was the child of an oral deaf mother who was apparently very successful in using spoken English. Bell also married an oral deaf woman, whom he had tutored. His father was a famous phonetician who had spent a considerable amount of time trying to develop aids for the deaf. There is a supposition that Alexander Graham Bell was trying to invent a hearing aid when he accidentally invented the telephone but there is no evidence for this, although some of the component parts of the telephone are also found in the hearing aid. The electronic hearing aid did not come into being until fifty years after the development of the telephone.

In 1880, educators of the deaf from all over the world convened in Milan, Italy, for an international congress to debate and discuss the methodology issue. Edward Miner Gallaudet, who was then the president of the Deaf-Mute College in Washington, DC (later to become known as Gallaudet University), read a paper defending the simultaneous method. After much debate, the following statement was issued:

> The Congress
>> considering that the simultaneous use of speech and signs has the disadvantage of injuring speech, lipreading and the precision of ideas,
> Declares—
>> that the pure oral method ought to be preferred.

This resolution passed overwhelmingly.

Oralism became the predominant educational philosophy during the first half of the twentieth century.

There were still schools, such as the American School, which used the *simultaneous method*, but they were a distinct minority. In 1965, the Federal Government commissioned a study of education of the deaf. The resulting Babbidge report was named after the study's chairman who was the president of the University of Connecticut and had no prior knowledge of deafness. Looking at education of the deaf with an unprejudiced eye, he concluded his report with the statement that educators of the deaf had nothing to be proud of. He went on to document the results of several studies that indicated that deaf people were notoriously underachieving. The vast majority of them were working in blue collar jobs with minimal academic and oral English skills. Over ninety percent of deaf people married other deaf people, and the goal of oralism to "normalize" the deaf was a distinct failure.

The report became the impetus for a revolution in education of the deaf. Total communication was developed to satisfy some of the objections of the oralists. By using a manually coded English system, it was hoped that the deaf would learn written and oral English. By also emphasizing hearing aids and speaking, it was hoped that children would develop good oral skills, and also satisfy the objection of the oralists.

In the 1960s, Owen Cornett developed cued speech. Because it was not language-based and required lipreading, cued speech was acceptable to many defecting oralists. Auralism also began in the 60s.

The roots of auralism go back to the 1930s. To have any success, auralism needed the technological development of the hearing aid to reach the loss and audiometers to measure residual hearing. For the first time, the hearing of deaf children could be tested with audiometric equipment. What the testers found was that the vast majority of deaf children (95%) had some residual hearing: this was startling to the investigators, as it had been assumed that deaf meant no hearing at all. (Many people still believe this.) With powerful amplification, some of the deaf children could be trained to use their hearing. This notion was developed by a remarkable otologist (most otologists don't concern themselves with educational issues) by the name of Max Goldstein, who wrote *The Acoustic Method* in 1939. This book promoted the idea of using amplification to utilize the residual hearing of deaf children. Auralism, in order to flower, still needed audiologists, who didn't come on the scene until the late 1940s. Audiology became involved with the nonmedical rehabilitation of the hearing impaired population. At first, the profession of audiology was devoted mainly to working with hard-of-hearing adults. A bit later, audiologists developed an interest in working with children and many became involved in developing instrumentation for the detection of hearing losses in children and in early habitation programs. A basic belief of the auralist is that children must use amplification very early in order for the approach to succeed. Hearing really takes place in the brain. The ear is just a transformer converting acoustic energy into neural energy. The brain needs to be trained to use the information supplied by the ear. This is why deaf children seldom respond right away to a hearing aid—they must have considerable auditory training. The earlier the training takes place, the better.

The revolution in special education came to the fore in the 1960s when minority groups, including disabled populations, began to assert their independence. This was certainly true of the deaf community, which was horrified by the manually coded English that they saw as a pollution of their language and another imposition by hearing people on the deaf community. They had felt oppressed for years by hearing educators of the deaf, who were preaching the benefits and virtues of oralism, while in reality most of the deaf persons were experiencing underemployment and social isolation. The deaf revolution culminated in 1988 with the fight over the presidency of Gallaudet College in Washington, DC. An insensitive Board of Trustees dominated by hearing people had nominated a hearing person for the presidency of Gallaudet. Up to that point, all the presidents of the university had been hearing. This time there was a revolt; the students went on strike and deaf people from all over the world came to protest. They forced the resignation of the nominee and subsequent appointment of the first deaf president of the university. This was, I think, the watershed of the deaf revolution. There are now many militant deaf people who are extremely active in the deaf community; they deplore "hearing" and are proud to be deaf.

ASL as a language and as an approach to educating deaf children has achieved educational legitimacy. Several schools that formerly used total communication are now bi-lingual/bi-cultural schools. (There are two in Massachusetts.) This means that ASL is taught and used almost exclusively in the preschool years to establish a language base. In elementary school, there is a switch to a signed English system in the hope that the students will develop competency in written English. To date, no definitive study has determined whether or not this approach will yield significantly better results in terms of academic achievement than other methods of educating deaf children. What bi/bi education has done is instill pride in deafness, and it has given deaf adults some control over the education of deaf children. Many teachers of this approach are deaf themselves.

A study conducted in 1985 indicated that the vast majority of schools for the deaf were using total communication: about 15% were oral/aural schools and very small minority (about 1%) were using cued speech. Since then, educators of the deaf have become increasingly disenchanted with the results of total communication.[6] Despite the fact that we have had twenty years of this approach, there has not been an appreciable improvement in the academic achievement scores of deaf children, which still remain depressingly low. Part of the difficulty may be in the nature of the signal presented in total communication. In bilingual homes, the child is presented with one language at a time and he or she is able to adapt to each language. In total communication, both languages, oral and manual sign, are presented simultaneously, and this may be very confusing for the child. The child may be receiving both an inadequate oral English signal and an inadequate signing input. We do know that in receiving information, one signal tends to predominate in the brain; this is known as the *figure*, while all other inputs are the *ground*. In total communication, it may be very hard for the child to determine what is the figure and what is the ground, causing inadequate language learning. This may be a case where more equals less.

In the meantime, auralism has been in the ascendancy. Children going the aural route are often educated outside of schools for the deaf, mainstreamed with normally hearing children. Association with other deaf children is usually discouraged. These children are generally seen in individual therapy and mainstreamed at the preschool level. For those children who cannot be mainstreamed directly there are small oral/auditory classes, but the goal is to place the deaf child in the mainstream eventually.

A study of aural adolescent hearing-impaired children[7] indicates that nearly forty percent had academic achievements on a par with normally hearing children. Many of these children also had very intelligible speech. The average reading level was eighth grade; while still behind the normal-hearing child, this result was considerably better than the fourth grade reading level of most other studies. These mainstreamed children may escape the scrutiny of investigators because they are often not in any established program for the deaf. The data on their superior academic achievement are not included in the depressingly low statistics that are consistently reported in studies of deaf children.

The studies comparing auditory/oral children with total communication children must be looked at with caution. Children in TC programs in schools for the deaf tend to have less hearing, to be of lower socioeconomic classes, and to have more concomitant problems than mainstreamed auditory/oral children. The studies are very difficult to compare because they are often looking at children with different backgrounds.

For parents of a newly diagnosed deaf child, the data on deaf children's academic achievements are really pretty meaningless: in the first place, there is a wide range of scores, and for every depressingly low one there is a startlingly high one. (No parent has an average child any way.) You are a unique experiment of one and the data are really not useful in helping you decide because they may not apply to your case. You can always find an example of a family who has been successful with each of the methods described. Any program will be able to trot out a successful child for you to see. (All programs, in addition to wanting more children, try to make parents feel better.)

The second point about the studies is that they are already obsolete by the time you examine them. The data are often accumulated on teenage children whose education experiences will not match your child's.

There has been an enormous amount happening in the past twenty years in education of the deaf that was not available to the parents and the children in the studies. Hearing aids are so much better, we hope we are doing a better job in parent education, and we are making much earlier identification than we were twenty years ago because of neonatal screening programs. There also may be more programs available now than there were for those parents and children reported on in those studies. While it is important for parents to know what has been done in the past, the studies must be taken with a grain of salt.

At the present time the auditory/aural approach is rapidly gaining ascendency. Present day hearing-impaired children are being identified at birth or shortly thereafter, fit with sophisticated hearing aids and, if they are not satisfactory, a cochlear implant is being provided. Relatively few families are now opting for bi/bi education. These programs are tending to revert to educating children from disadvantaged homes, multiply handicapped deaf, or deaf children of deaf parents. Although the present day hearing-impaired child has a much better chance of developing better oral and English language skills than the child of the past, I am not sure he or she is any happier. These children have to confront identity problems and problems related to social acceptance; they are children under stress, and social and educational structures have not evolved yet to help them. Parents are going to have to monitor these children carefully and in many cases be the architects of the needed social programs.

Education of very young deaf children is largely an input problem—language has to be learned from someone in the environment. The best people to do this are the parents, usually the mother (and that is why language is referred to as the mother tongue). The decision the parents must make is how to put the language in. These are the choices they have: (1) use oral English with encouragement to the child to look; (2) oral English with an emphasis on listening; (3) American Sign Language; (4) a manually coded English system with speech; or (5) a cued speech system. At this time, it seems that education of the deaf is being polarized by the auralists on one hand, and the ASL deaf community on the other. I don't know whether the center will hold.

It is beyond the scope of this book to get into the issues in language learning and language teaching. Suffice it to say that teaching language to a deaf child, irrespective of methodology, is an input problem. Emphasis in teaching, as with a normally hearing child, must be on helping the child to understand the linguistic signal by providing him or her with many concrete examples of the linguistic signal and the event or object being described. For the deaf child, we need to present many more examples than we would to a normally hearing child; output by the child, whether it be by sign or by speech, is the last step in the language learning process. Parents must learn to be patient. It takes what seems like forever for the child to finally begin speaking or begin signing. There is a lot of hard work involved. An excellent chapter by Ellen Kurtzer-White in *The Young Deaf Child*[8] describes in detail the process of beginning speech and language habilitation with the very young hearing-impaired child.

In the Emerson program we give parents a choice of method. I don't think any method will work unless the parents commit themselves to it. You make a commitment when you do the choosing: we are defined in life by the choices we make.

We also believe that the child will tell you how he or she wants to learn. After observing deaf children for a while we see that some are visual learners who want and can use the unambiguous signal provided by a sign system. Other children are able to use their residual hearing very well, and even though the audiogram indicates that they have minimal hearing, they seem able to use every bit of it. Audiologists tend to classify children on the basis of audiograms, sending very deaf children to total communication programs and hard-of-hearing children to auditory/oral programs. I think this is a mistake; while hearing is important, it isn't the sole determinant of aural success. We have seen children with very severe losses do quite well aurally while other children with more pure tone hearing don't do nearly as well. I think what is needed is a period of experimental teaching to find which is the best method for your child. There is no one method that is suitable for all children. The method must be tailored to the deaf child rather than trying to tailor the child to the method.

At the Emerson program, we do not offer parents bi-lingual/bi-cultural education because I think this is too difficult an option for hearing parents of newly diagnosed deaf children to utilize. It means that parents must learn a whole new language at a time when they are emotionally distraught. I don't think that is a feasible burden for most hearing parents of newly diagnosed deaf children to bear. Deaf parents, on the other hand, may be able to use this approach effectively.

I also have some philosophical qualms about educating very young deaf children in ASL, which minimizes the use of amplification and devalues speech; I think it is limiting. It is educating deaf children to function in a very restricted environment. With a pure ASL approach, we may be creating a generation of deaf adults who will be angry at their parents and teachers for not encouraging them to speak: and so it goes. I think it is unrealistic to expect more than a handful of hearing people to become proficient in ASL, and I think that in order to compete vocationally in "the hearing world," deaf children need to be equipped with some oral skills. The ASL approach also goes against the underlying culture of the United States, which is to integrate minorities into the melting pot of our culture while at the same time respecting cultural differences. (I suspect the militant move for a separate deaf society will fade, much the way we do not hear the call for a black nation anymore. As a repressed minority group reaches maturity, it recognizes the need to integrate to some extent into the larger society.) There is, I think, a very reasonable middle course to take. According to my good friend, Jack Roush,[9]

> What most deaf adults want is the same thing as the rest of us seek in our personal, social, and religious endeavors; others with whom we can enjoy relaxed and effective communication. Because a Polish-American chooses to socialize, worship or marry other Poles does not mean he or she is a member of a "separate society." I think it is healthier to think of the deaf community as a "linguistic minority" or ethnic subculture rather than as a disability group. Not to say that deafness is not disabling at times; like a physical disability, it's "situation specific." I see no harm in "deaf pride" if it improves self-esteem.

I feel very strongly, however, that the goal of educating the young deaf child has to be to give the child as many options as possible and then to respect the choices he or she eventually makes. In order to give the child choices, we must give him or her every opportunity to learn speech and this can be done best by encouraging the use of residual hearing early in the child's education.

The bi/bi message of deafness as a separate culture is a hard one for hearing parents of newly diagnosed deaf children to hear because they are not of that culture. At the present time, there seems to be minimal contact between hearing parents of deaf children and the deaf community. I think this is a loss.

Our policy in the Emerson program is that if parents opt for ASL, we will refer them elsewhere. I cannot, in good conscience, use this approach with a young, deaf child. Try as I might, I still see deafness as a disability that can be overcome or certainly minimized with the appropriate use of technology, appropriate methodology, and careful parent education. Nevertheless, there is much that the deaf community has to offer to both the parents and the deaf child. I think every parent needs to meet and relate to deaf adults. Their experiences need to be heard—the mistakes of the past must not be repeated. Deaf children also need to see and to have deaf adults as positive role models.

In addition to my misgivings about bi/bi, I also have a great deal of difficulty with the auralists. I think they often achieve impressive speech and academic results with the children but at a very high cost in terms of the sheer hard work and frustration for both the child and the parents. Auralism is based on a denial of deafness that can be psychologically unhealthy. There is a great deal of isolation in the approach; the deaf child needs a peer group to relate to and parents need other parents to share experiences with. We have found that many seemingly successfully mainstreamed oral/aural children who had graduated from our program eventually opted to go to deaf college programs because they were very tired of working twice as hard in order to keep up with their hearing peers. These are children who were highly stressed and not very happy. Because they were also often socially isolated, they eagerly sought out the deaf community to relate to. In fact, many of the leaders of the deaf community and leading proponents of the bi/bi movement, were formerly very successful oral children who were "turned off" by the constant push for the hearing world and rebelled against their parents and teachers.

The results of our twenty-five year survey indicate that parents who opted for an aural/oral education for their child were happier with their child's academic success and speech than parents who had chosen a total communication approach. On the other hand, the aural parents were less happy with their child's social adjustment than the parents of the TC children. A typical example was that of one mother who wrote of her deaf daughter:

> Susan is a very lovely girl who went through our local elementary and high school. Her grades were good throughout, but she had no real friends. She used to come home and study and the phone never rang. No one took her to the prom. She went one year to B_____ College and made the Dean's List. But she couldn't take the isolation and sheer hard work anymore. The next year she transferred to NTID (National Technical Institute for the Deaf) and has been very happy ever since. She now signs and has a boyfriend who is also deaf.

Another mother wrote about her son's school experience.

> On the surface he seems happy; at a deeper level he has great anger about events in his life, experiences great isolation, and is not part of the hearing world really and certainly not any part at all of any deaf world.

The message of the deaf community must be heeded: children need access to that community. I think all deaf children should learn sign language; some should get it very early in their schooling, while others should get it later. In the Emerson program we offer parents a combined aural/TC alternative. We have found, contrary to what the strict auralists preach, that exposure to other deaf children and a little exposure to sign language do not prevent a deaf child from establishing good aural/oral skills. In our nursery, we mix the TC children with the aural children while signing only with the TC children. The aural children are exposed to signs, too, but indirectly. We find that a bit of sign seems to enhance the development of speech and language in very aural children. Many parents start out by signing: when the child has the word established, they drop the sign. (This may be a better way to do total communication.)

To be successful in educating a deaf child, the parents (and the professional) must steer a narrow course. One can embrace the best of auralism without denying the child's deafness and, for those deaf children who are visually inclined, one can take the best of total communication while still equipping the child to move comfortably in the hearing world. To sign with a deaf child does not necessarily mean the child will not speak well, and to be aural with a child does not necessarily mean the self-esteem will be low. It is a very tricky course parents have to follow. They have to be alert to changes in the child's needs and changes in the educational plan.

No educational plan should be more than one year in duration. Children's needs change and programs change. It is never a mistake to place your child in a program that does not work out as long as you change the program when you realize its limitations. At that point you have valuable information; it is a mistake only if you do it a second time. Another way of saying this is that a mistake occurs only if you haven't learned anything.

In my experience, parents make the mistake of staying too long with a program after they have realized it is not a fruitful route to take. Parents persist because they are afraid to admit a mistake or because they are fearful of the stress of trying to find a new program (They are also often helped by a biased professional who counsels them to wait.) It seems easier to stay than to begin anew the search for a more suitable program or method. Fortunately for us, education of the deaf is not like brain surgery: we can afford to explore various alternatives and make "mistakes." Also fortunately for us, children are sturdy and can survive our blunders.

Parents must become the countervailing force to the child's program; you must complement the program. Many aural/auditory programs place heavy academic demands on the child, and he or she is often exhausted after a full day in school. Parents must then be relaxed with the child. It would be a mistake to try to teach lessons at home when the child needs some relief and time out. Total communication programs, on the other hand, tend to be more relaxed than aural programs and have had a somewhat lower academic standard. (This varies at times with the teacher, not necessarily the method.) With these programs the parents can afford to provide more intellectual stimulation at home. the parents' role for the school-age deaf child is to provide a holistic program by complementing what goes on in school.

Parents of hearing-impaired children, must assume the role of program monitor. It is essential that they not take anything for granted; they must always see to it that the child is making progress and they must be willing to make adjustments when necessary.

At times being the monitor of your child's program means you must be his or her advocate. this will put you in opposition to the professionals. There are times when you must be thought of as unreasonable and not afraid to be regarded as a "pushy parent." Professionals are often constrained by budget limitations and professional inertia. You are less constrained and often can come up with innovative solutions that do not limit the child, although they may stretch the school's budget and the professional's imagination. One mother had the following dream:

> I was leading the parade dressed in combat boots, battle fatigues and a sword at my side carrying a flag to the beat of a military march. Behind me came my daughter.

Often it may feel this way to you as you do battle to see that your child gets the best break possible. But if you don't do it, who will?

THE HARD-OF HEARING CHILD

Throughout this book, I have used the term *deaf* child. I recognize that there are many more hard-of-hearing children than deaf children (about fifteen times as many). Many of the problems of parents of deaf children are the same for parents of hard-of-hearing children. The grief process is the same for both; because your child may hear a bit better than a deaf child does not help you in the grieving stages. It is still a loss of the dream and it still means that parents will have to be "special." Although this is not always appreciated by your family, friends, and the professionals who are busy telling you that "it could be so much worse he could be *deaf*" and thereby not giving you permission to grieve your loss, the truth of the matter is that the hearing loss is not in the audiogram but in the perception of the loss, and for you it is often a bad loss no matter what others may be telling you.

There will also be a great deal of stress on the whole family system. The degree of hearing loss makes no difference in these respects. Where there is a difference is in the educational planning. A hard-of-hearing child, or even a deaf one who is functionally hard of hearing, is clearly an oral child who will most likely be mainstreamed. This is the potential and this may be the curse because the problems that the hard-of-hearing child has are more subtle than those of the deaf child and are not always apparent to professionals who don't have experience with hearing loss or family members who are in denial.

Hard-of-hearing children usually have subtle language problems, and consequently, academic problems. Many of them learn to be good fakers and head nodders and they can slip between the cracks. Teachers do not always appreciate the dimensions of their loss. Their hearing appears to be inconsistent because they have difficulty when the classroom is noisy and hear quite well when it is quiet. They usually can hear some pitches of sounds quite well and some very poorly. They are frequently accused of not paying attention. Because they have to be alert all of the time in the classroom, they may become fatigued and irritable. They are often not understood and may be misdiagnosed as having an attention deficit disorder or as being emotionally disturbed. Very often they have a negative educational experience and become underachievers despite normal or above average intelligence.

Socially, it is not easy to be hard of hearing either. There are no national organizations promoting help for the hard-of-hearing child as there are for other disability groups. (There is a group for adult hearing-impaired people called S.H.H.H., Self Help for the Hard of Hearing. As yet they have no child component.) These children do not have access to the deaf community; they are viewed as hearing by the deaf community and are generally not accepted. Their communicative problems and orientation toward the world are generally more like hearing persons than deaf ones. It becomes difficult for hard-of-hearing children to find peer groups that will accept them. They find it difficult to keep up with hearing children and are generally not happy among deaf people either. All in all, it is a formidable problem that is not always appreciated. While parents in our support group who have hard-of-hearing children generally feel lucky as compared to the parents of deaf children, they don't really appreciate the kinds of problems they are going to encounter.

This is also becoming true for children who are successfully using cochlear implants. They become "hard-of-hearing" deaf children within the mainstream, and despite the help they get from the implant they are still "deaf," and experience the isolation and stress that any mainstreamed hearing-impaired child undergoes.

I know that the methodology issue and the school placement issue are formidable ones that cause parents many sleepless nights. I think it almost doesn't matter what method you select, as long as you find a good teacher who is committed to teaching, enthusiastic about your child, sensitive to his or her needs, and consistent in the application of method. We all have to be clear in our definition of success. For me, success is measured by the child's capacity for joy in living and the ability to have satisfactory personal relationships. In short, I want people to be glad this child is alive. I want all children to develop to their potential and to be as productive as possible. All else is relatively unimportant.

For me, oral skills are much too narrow a gauge of success. To be truly successful in life, you must like yourself. One thing you can always be sure of: as long as you are conscious, you will have to live with yourself. So, you might as well live with a winner. A major source of our self-esteem is how our parents feel about us—as was said earlier in this book and needs to be repeated here, parents are like a mirror to their child and the child needs to see a beautiful person reflected back to him or her. This means the parents must come to love the deafness because it is such an integral part of the child. You must see the deafness not as a terrible deficit, but as the powerful teacher that it is. You must learn to embrace the hearing loss as you embrace your child.

Hearing loss does not preclude a productive and good life. David Wright, a deaf poet, has this to say about disability:

> The handicapped are less at the mercy of the vague unhappiness that afflicts so many, especially those without aim in life, whose consequent boredom promotes what used to be called spleen. The disabled have been given a built-in, ready-packed objective, an objective which is always present; a definite impediment to get the better of. Like the prospect of hanging, it concentrates the facilities wonderfully (p.111)[10]

CHAPTER 8

Parent to Parent

This chapter is written entirely by parents of deaf children. As mentioned in the Introduction, I surveyed all the parents who had gone through the nursery as we prepared to celebrate its twenty-fifth anniversary, and selected material from parents of children 6 to 25 years-of-age. I have edited the material lightly and arranged it within the chapter to read easily. All of the parents responded to the survey question that asked what advice they would give to the parents of a newly diagnosed deaf child.

Relax! Enjoy your child as a child, not just as being hearing impaired. Get the most out of each program that your child is in and be the best advocate for your child in each situation. Educate yourself as much as possible and enjoy each program your child is involved in. Your child will let you know when he or she is ready to move on.

1. Get support . . . parent group/sibling group/early intervention programs.
2. Check out many different kinds of programs/philosophies—keep an open mind. After you sift through it all, you will know what is best for your

child and if it doesn't work out . . . change it . . . make it work.

3. Become a child advocate. Don't expect anyone to take you by the hand and do the work for you—it won't happen. Educate yourself. Be assertive. Learn the law and the rights of your child.

4. I remember when Todd was diagnosed. It was like someone put this 18-month-old baby on my lap and said, "We want you to raise this baby in his native tongue, culture, and educate him in a different kind of way—by the way, we want you to learn language, but the experts are still arguing what is right (oral/TC). And if you chose TC, experts are arguing what is correct (English/ASL)." But *You* have to know now and make decisions now! And this is during the most upsetting year of your life anyway! I wanted someone to take care of me and my child, and show me what was the right thing to do.

5. Don't forget your family! I have always felt the ones who suffer the most are the siblings—importance shifted to the deaf child. Spend special time with your hearing children. Take time out to go out with your husband—you both need a break, *and* each other.

The pain of the discovery never really goes away, but it does dull. Look at your child very well and make your decisions based on his abilities and not your desires. Always remember that they are normal children in all ways except for their ability to hear.

I would tell them to meet my sons. Keep your eyes ahead so your child will learn to look toward a future.

Don't drive yourself crazy; just really get to know your child as a child. Then learn about education and all the things *you need* to know about deafness. Don't forget to ask for help.

Get educated! Visit grown-up deaf teens and talk to their parents. Go to seminars and see what is happening in the "deaf world." Also, love your child, in spite of his or her deafness, and learn to sign. Invite their friends over and accept your child's deafness and also his deaf friends. Get involved with his or her school.

Eat well, develop exercise habits, turn off the TV, talk with each other, and relax.

Don't waste time feeling sorry for yourself or your child. Try to get your child in a good program as soon as possible and learn how to work with him or her—to constantly talk to him or her, etc. Pretty much what I learned at Emerson. Find a group of other parents of deaf children. It is extremely helpful. Have high goals for your child, as they can do more than you think possible. Most important—*Love Them* for who they are.

Trust yourself as a parent. You know your child better than any professional. Listen carefully to what others —laymen and professionals—say, look at yourself and your family needs, and make the decisions you need to make for your child.

✍

Deal with the deafness—get the support you need to help your child make his way in life. Above all, see beyond the deafness to the child himself. Know how much he can accomplish and help him to do that—as a complete person.

✍

Do not be a crutch for them. Always remember that these are our children *First*, and that the "handicap" is secondary. Both parents must get involved in their child's learning experiences and education.

✍

You have to go through a mourning period, but try to get a support system going so that you can get on with your life and help yourself, your child, and your entire family unit. Visiting programs, meeting other parents, and reading were very helpful in working through our grief. Dave Luterman is a unique counselor, friend, and educator. Seek him out!

✍

Remember that you have a young person there for you to take care of. Don't ever let the deafness get in the way of your love for this child. In the end, if you remember this, the fruits of all the love and acceptance will come back to you triplefold. You will have a person who is deaf, who likes himself or herself because you have set the example of acceptance. Others will follow your example. The added frosting is that you will have a person who is capable of giving and receiving love. They will never feel they don't deserve to be loved. They will realize that no matter how smart you are, how beautiful you are on the outside, etc., if people don't like you, the opportunities won't be there for you. Help your child become a person that people like and respect.

1. Give them a goal of self-image.
2. Talk, talk, talk.
3. Teach, teach, teach.
4. Pray, pray, pray.
5. Talk to deaf adults who have "made it."
6. Aim high—be realistic about their ability, but don't lower your expectations because of this handicap.
7. Fight, fight, fight for them. Don't accept second-best from the "professionals" (you have to be diplomatic, but get your point across).
8. Separate what may be his or her own innate personality from his or her deafness. Learn the difference between the behavior because it's *Them* and the behavior because he or she is hearing impaired.

Dig, dig, dig. There is a lot of help out there, but it does not come on a silver platter! We have met some wonderful people along the way.

Get to know yourself and your child. Observing your child in different situations will teach you more about him or her and his or her needs than any professional in the field of deafness. This will help you deal with conflicting advice. Life's going to be tough, so relax, enjoy your child, and acquire a sense of humor, if you don't have one. When faced with the decisions you're going to have to make, always follow your "gut feelings" or you may lose your child to someone else's idea of what's best.

Just take one day at a time and do whatever is needed
to make the child happy and well-adjusted.

Visit different schools, go to meetings, read everything,
especially *Silent Voices* by Oliver Sachs. Get counseling, meet and associate with deaf adults and children,
get a deaf babysitter or mother's helper, have deaf children from school over to play, go to deaf camp for a
visit, attend sign language courses, have a deaf oral or
ASL adult come to visit, go to MPAD [Massachusetts
Parents Association of the Deaf or you own state asso-
ciation] fairs, contact vocational educational counselors for the deaf, get a good picture of your child's
learning style and needs.

It is important for the child to have some other friends
with hearing impairments. Go to Emerson first.

1. Therapy. You don't realize until later what the effect of this is—it is absolutely profound. I've done
   an awful lot of work, mostly on my own, and I
   wish I had realized I needed more help. It would
   have been easier.
2. Get into a parents' support group: not the kind
   that does lobbying and fund-raising (although
   that's important down the road), but the kind with
   no professionals. You need to form a bond with
   others in your shoes.
   "Loneliness is a longing for kind, not a longing for company."
3. Keep a sharp eye on your other children. They do
   not come through this unscathed! It may take

many years for the effects to show, but they will show. Parents should know that, through no fault of anyone's they are now living in a "dysfunctional" family, and their other children will react to that. The sooner we accept this fact, the better we'll deal with it. If not, our kids will act out or be controlled super-kids—neither one is healthy.

4. Recognize that you're the mom and dad, not therapist or teacher. It's important to follow through with the child's program in order to maintain consistency, but the child needs unconditional love and parenting from you, *not* a 24-hour school day.

5. Finally I'd like to put in a plug for signing. I'm not going to address the controversy, but I think new parents should be made aware that signing and total communication may be a more viable language system for their child than speech. There is nothing wrong with enrolling in a signing class. It makes you aware of the existence of the deaf community and of deaf culture, which is probably going to be a reality in your life at some point. Also, it gives new parents something constructive to do. We want to feel that there's something we can do. Besides the initial feelings of anger, guilt, sorrow, etc., there is an enormous feeling of helplessness. Learning to sign is concrete.

Sign language is essential at some point in time.

Keep your wits about you—this is not something to get hysterical about. It can be more an irritant than a problem if you use your energy to learn everything you can about deafness, special education laws, deaf education, all modes of communication, your child's own case, and you know what you want and where you want the child to be when he or she is 18 or 21 years old. What are your goals? How do you get there?

✍️

The deafness is never going to go away. The family's collective energy is better spent on making the deafness a normal part of the family experience than crying about why he or she isn't normal.

✍️

1. Get into a group with other parents of the deaf. Be sure the group is monitored by someone who can handle the emotional dynamics of parents of deaf children.
2. Learn all you can about deafness from every perspective—talking, reading, sharing, etc.
3. Believe in your child as normal, having a hearing impairment.
4. Have the same expectations of your deaf child as you do your hearing child.
5. Relax and have fun.
6. If you want to cry, do it (but not in front of the child).
7. If you want to get mad at the situation, do it! It gets rotten sometimes!
8. Don't blame your spouse.
9. Be sure you and your spouse talk about your feelings to each other.
10. Be there for one another.
11. Get away once in a while because a handicapped child can use up much time and energy.
12. Commit yourselves to your child's independence by becoming self-reliant.
13. Adopt a communication skill(s) the child is best suited for.

14. Be consistent in attitude, expectations, and respect!

✍

I think *Real* total communication (only if speech is included for real) is the best way to go. Almost every deaf person I know now is more relaxed with signs, but I still want to have the opportunity to try to reach the limits of the child's oral experience.

✍

There still needs to be a lot of education to the hearing world. In the last three years, I can't believe the ignorance we have seen.

✍

Place the child in a program at as early an age as possible to develop communication—preferably *Total*.

✍

Seek out David Luterman (or a clone) and listen to everything he says to you. Heed the advice of professionals, talk about it, and have confidence in your child.

✍

Don't sit back and accept everything the professionals tell you about how to educate your child or his or her potential for the future. Do your own research. Speak to anyone who may be of help. Make educated decisions.
Must read books: *Choices in Deafness*, Sue Schwartz
Learning To Listen, Pat Vaughan

✍

Give yourself time to absorb the news. Get involved in a support group. Deal with your own feelings on the deafness. Get the child into a program of some kind, and don't be afraid to change if you think you're not going anywhere with your child.

✍

Try both sign language and total communication. We're both convinced our child is better off today because of that route.

✍

Don't despair. There is a world out there into which your child will fit very well. Love and know your child and have confidence in that knowledge. The most important contribution you can make is to enable your child to feel good about him or herself and to take an active part in every aspect of your child's development. Make sure your child's educational experience is designed to allow him or her to reach his or her individual maximum potential. Most of all, enjoy your child as a child.

✍

Fathers view: Listen to group discussions at first, but I think that gets old after a while. The main thing is to do what you know in your heart is the best thing to do. The parents are the only ones that know their child. Books, doctors, and specialists can give you advice, but what they tell you is not as good as what you learn as time goes by.

Mothers view: I feel parents have to put their child first before everything. As your child grows, you, as parents, grow also. The culture of the deaf is wonderful. Be willing to let the child become part of the deaf culture even though we, as hearing, will not be able to. You must be willing to drive miles to get to friends' houses and different happenings in the deaf world. Do not get locked into a program and think that if it's fine for them now, it will always be fine. Children change and it is very hard to pull your child out of a program, but if it's not working any longer, you, as the parent, must change it. Keep up with what is happening at the school: ask your child, talk to the teacher and other parents. Make sure your child gets what he or she is supposed to get. Just because it's written in an I.E.P., does not mean it is done at the school. You must be the one to make sure it's done, and if it's not being done, you must fight for it.

I have met many people who believe that what is in the I.E.P. is being done at school and never check. Too many parents put their child into a program and never look to make sure it's working. It may work for now, but as the children get older, they need different things.

Our school had no parent group and no sign class for the children until a mother and I started one. It took two years before it went smoothly. Now we are starting a group for parents of deaf children in Massachusetts who want socialization for their children.

Have the same hopes and goals for the deaf child as you would have for a hearing child. I could go on forever. I have learned a lot in my past ten years of being a parent of a deaf child.

✍

Giving my children all options such as speech, lipreading, and ASL, and treating them no different from my other child has made them strong, independent children. Also, by not dwelling on the fact that my children are severely hearing-impaired and possibly deaf in the future, my children are happy, playful little girls who are socially accepted by both hearing and deaf children. I believe they have the best of both worlds.

Attempt to become as knowledgeable as possible about deafness. Be involved in your child's education. Don't be afraid of educators. Remember he or she is *your* child.

Accept them as they are, but encourage them to work to the maximum of their potential. *Love* your child! Do not resent his or her handicap. You, as the parent, know him or her best. Listen to the experts, but follow your feelings and convictions. Encourage the child's independence; *do not* swaddle or overprotect them. Allow them to express themselves, but be sure to give them the parental guidance they need. If your child wants to try something alone, *let* him or her. Do not let family members influence your thinking: this includes grandparents, older bothers and sisters, and aunts and uncles. Even if they have experienced a deaf child, they have not experienced *your* deaf child.

Every situation is different. Listen to the advice of others but you, as parents, must make the appropriate choices and/or decisions.

I would tell them to instill confidence and independence in their children and to give them an abundance of love and affection. They should learn to sign. Also, when you speak to your child, speak normally with no baby talk; use complete sentences and correct grammar. Look into all the programs for the hearing-impaired and choose the one you feel would be best suited for your child. Talk with other parents of deaf children. Also, read material about deafness.

Don't lose heart. Examine all options. Keep stimulating your child by talk, talk, talk! Be aware that it is important for the child to listen.

1. Have marriage counseling all along the way! You are now at risk for divorce—face it and prevent it. Don't let your partner beg out of involvement with the child, the process, and the healing.
2. Work hard— there's no time to lose. The time for language acquisition will pass.
3. Treat him or her like a normal kid—he or she is.
4. Learn that you need a hard heart when he or she acts out and a soft heart to comfort. Neither one will do all the time. The trick is to know when for which.

View your child as an individual. Don't accept preconceived limitations. Be consistent in training speech therapy.

Talk about your feelings, listen to professionals, act cautiously about future plans for your children, but remember, if mistakes or wrong decisions are made, they can always be changed.

Continually evaluate your child's abilities and educational experience. If they have the ability to be aural, give them the opportunity.

✍

Treat your child as a normal child—make good educational decisions and know that it's the very best you know how to do at that moment in time. Have hope, for there is much good help out there. If your child has good voice quality, teach him to speak as well as possible; if he or she doesn't have understandable speech, then teach him or her and give him or her every tool to communicate. Deal with your own feelings about the deafness and come to a peaceful state about it. Teach your child to have self esteem; it's the single most valuable gift you can give. Find a support system for your child if he or she needs it.

✍

Take things as slowly as you can tolerate. The children have to evolve in their own time and their own way. They will give clues as to what they need. Also, the deafness is only one part of their lives. For the children, it is quite normal. Finally, talk to other parents and let yourself believe that the feelings of anger, fear, sadness, etc., are okay and need to be dealt with. It won't help the child if the parents are in emotional chaos.

✍

Believe in yourself and your child. Follow your gut feelings. Learn from other parents about what worked for them, and be willing to try different approaches. Be willing to put your heart, soul, money, and time into your child, and you will be rewarded. Expect the best from your child. Be persistent. Set high goals and help your child attain them. Learn all you can. Always see your child as a child first (instead of a deaf child). Share your experiences with other parents. Give your child many opportunities to learn. Be willing to try new things (who could have guessed she would be the best dancer in her ballet class?!).

Being the parent of a newly diagnosed deaf child is not as bad or as hard as it used to be. The opportunity for success is vast, even if it's different from what your expectations originally were.

Get help fast. I would definitely encourage parents to give the child the opportunity to learn to speak and to develop residual hearing. Parents should encourage the child to participate in activities, both group and individual. Clarke School helped to develop a good self-image. Also, and perhaps very important, do not allow the excuse, "I can't do it because I am deaf." Try hard and never give up—that is what makes a deaf child successful.

1. Always remember that your child is deaf and sooner or later you must be the one to tell him. Remember always to hold your head high in public places and never be ashamed of deafness. Meaning, in McDonald's for example . . . your deaf child is talking too loudly or signing and all eyes are upon you and his siblings . . . remember to inform the siblings that they will always be stared at during the brother's life because of the deafness. In the meantime, hold your head high and continue talking and signing to your deaf child. In private conversation, tell your other children they will always be on display in grocery stores, banks, libraries, etc., and then the entire family will cope with deafness and its acceptance.

2. When old enough, tell your child not to bang the toilet seat or slam the bathroom door or not to ring the doorbell 3,000 times because that will disturb hearing people. This comes in very handy, especially when Grandma comes to visit and continually asks why your child is banging everything. Remember that Grandma does not really understand deafness, and probably never will . . . don't waste a lot of time on people trying to explain deafness, because most people truly do not understand the concept—make it short and sweet when explaining, and phrase it in grammar-school English so that people will understand you. For example, do not go on about nerve loss, decibel level, intricacy of hearing aids; use that valuable time talking to your child, having people talk to him or her "face to face," or use that time with your child talking about residual hearing and pointing out environmental sounds, always!

3. Get yourself a cheap Polaroid camera—you will never have enough film. Take a single picture of everyone in the family, not group pictures; put them on a rolodex, not a photo album because that's too busy for the deaf child to grasp. When Auntie Joan and Uncle John are coming to visit, you can remove only those pictures and show the child who is coming. Take pictures of the playground, the library, the doctor's office, the hearing aid dealer—anyone, so you can have visual aids to let your child know what is going to happen. Remember, being taken into a car, put into a car seat, strapped in, driving for one hour, walking into a tall building, and then having some man in a white coat look into your ears is very frightening; but with the picture, you can at least give an idea of the destination!

4. Purchase a coloring book that shows occupations such as a banker, dentist, doctor, construction

worker, etc. Color the book brightly for your child. Use this when going to the dentist. Remember, always let your child hold things. If your child wants to, he or she will hold the polaroid snapshot all the way to the market just to be sure in his mind that he is going to the market and not to see the ear doctor! Try not to change plans midstream, like getting into the car and deciding to stop at Joan's for three hours before going to the market. This is very confusing to the deaf child.

5. Try to lead a somewhat structured life, like brushing your teeth at the same time every day, eating meals at the same time, etc.

6. If you live in a town that has activities with other children available, such as fingerpainting at the library, take your child. Expose your child as much as possible to all children in your neighborhood. Remember her or she will be growing up there for many years, unless you move a lot. Do not try to hire a interpreter for everyday circumstances in which your child might participate, for example, if there might be a little day camp during the summer for toddlers or preschool kids. Do not teach your child at an early age that he will have an interpreter at all times in life. Let him wing it, and, sure, that is hard, but life is hard and no one will lay out the red carpet because you are deaf, remember that. If your child finds at a young age that it is a struggle to communicate with hearing people, you are conditioning him for the future. This is just as hard on the parents as on the child, believe me.

7. It is very important to find time alone for husband and wife, even if it means taking a cheap bottle of wine to the river and throwing down a blanket and just being together as a couple, and then spending

all the money you saved on the date to pay the babysitter. Also, do not fuss over the fact that your sitter does not sign and cannot communicate with your child. Be more involved with your child's safety when getting a sitter; one who can run after that deaf child and who is not too old to jump for that kid when needed. I have very seldom seen a slow deaf child.

8. Remember to play physically with your baby; romping, wrestling, roughhousing, rocking, touching, kissing, and just plain letting your hair down all help you enjoy him and help him enjoy his parents. Don't always be a speech therapist.

9. Remember to tell your deaf child, "I love you." It can be read on you lips, seen in your eyes, felt in your body, and seen in your body language.

Endnotes

1. Throughout this text, I use the terms "deaf" and "hearing impaired" interchangeably. By these terms, I mean any hearing loss that has a severe impact on a child's ability to learn language and speech.
2. Featherstone, H. 1980. *A Difference in the Family*, p. 232. Basic Books.
3. Published by permission of the author, Emily Perl Kingsley. Excerpted from the teleplay: *Kids Like These* by Emily Perl Kingsley and Alan E. Sloane. Produced for CBS Television by Nexus Publications, Inc. and Taft Entertainment. © All Rights Reserved.
4. Bender, R. 1960. *The Conquest of Deafness*. Cleveland, OH: Case Western Reserve University.
5. Musselman, C., P. Lindsay, and A. Wilson. 1988. An evaluation of recent trends in preschool programming for hearing impaired children. *Journal of Speech and Hearing Disorders*. 53:71–88.
6. Luterman, D. 1987. *Deafness in Perspective*. San Diego: College Hill Press.
7. Geers, J. and J. Moog. 1988. Factors predictive of the development of literacy in profoundly hearing-impaired adolescents. *The Volta Review*. 91(2):131–137.
8. Kurtzer-White, E., and Luterman, D. 2001. *The Young Deaf Child*. Baltimore: York Press, Inc.
9. Roush, J. Personal correspondence.
10. Wright, D. 1969. *Deafness*. New York: Stein & Day.

Appendix A
A Random Bibliography

The following are books that I have found helpful or that parents have suggested to me. There is no attempt to be definitive or exhaustive.

Featherstone, H. 1980. *A Difference in the Family.* New York: Basic Books.

A moving account of the mother of a severely disabled child. This is an extremely well-written, sensitive portrait of a family coping with severe disability. Featherstone is also a professional, so she is able to move in both the objective and subjective modes.

Forecki, M. 1985. *Speak to Me.* Washington, DC: Gallaudet College Press.

A well-written account of the mother of a six-year-old, very active deaf child. Written humorously and sensitively. It is a quite literate and candid book.

Jacobs, L. 1980. *A Deaf Man Speaks Out* #9 2nd Edition. Washington, DC: Gallaudet University Press.

A memoir of a deaf man raised by deaf parents who is also comfortable with his deafness and the deaf world.

Kisor, H. 1990. *What Is That Pig Outdoors?* New York: Hill & Wang.

Don't get thrown off by the weird title. This is a memoir written by a deaf man who was raised oral and is very comfortable with his deafness. Of note is the minimal amount of professional help his mother had, which may speak volumes.

Luterman, D. 2000. *The Young Deaf Child*. Baltimore: York Press.

This book contains a comprehensive history of education of the deaf, as well as discussions of issues in screening of newborns and programming for parents. A chapter by Seewald describes amplification systems and one by Kurtzer-White is on beginning speech and language development in a very young hearing impaired child. Intended for professionals, this book can be read by parents.

Schwartz, S. 1987. *Choices in Deafness*. Kensington, MD: Woodbine House.

A good, objective description of total communication, cued speech, and oralism. Alternate chapters are written by a professional describing the methodology and then by a parent using it. The tone of the writing sometimes seems patronizing and it, therefore, grates, but the book is full of very useful information.

Spradley, T., and Spradley, J. 1978. *Deaf Like Me*. New York: Random House.

A book written by angry parents who pursued for too long the oralist dream, only to discover their child needed sign language all along. An odyssey every parent needs to look at, if only to relearn the truth about trusting self and not always trusting professionals.

Walker, L. 1986. *A Loss for Words*. New York: Harper & Row.

The story of a hearing daughter of deaf parents. It is a sensitively told account of growing up hearing in the midst of deafness. It is very moving and poignant.

Appendix B
Organizations

Here are some useful organization you should know about.

A. G. Bell Association for the Deaf
3417 Volta Place, NW
Washington, DC 20007-2778

> Publishes the Volta Review and offers an array of books and magazines. This organization is primarily interested in promoting an auditory-aural philosophy.

American Annals of the Deaf
K. D. E. S. PAS-6800
Florida Avenue, NE
Washington, DC 20002

> Publishes the American Annals of the Deaf and is the official organization of the Convention of American Instructors of the Deaf. This organization and journal are very sign-oriented. Publishes an annual directory that lists all programs in the United States.

American Speech, Language and Hearing Association
10801 Rockville Pike
Rockville, MD 20852-3279

> Publishes the Journal of Speech and Hearing Disorders, certifies programs that train audiologists, and provides information for speech, language, and hearing impaired.

John Tracy Clinic
806 West Adams Boulevard
Los Angeles, CA 90007

> One of the first parent-centered programs established in the United States. It provides a free correspondence course for

parents to work at home with their child. A strong oral orientation.

Gallaudet University

7th Street and Florida Avenue, NE

Washington, DC 20002

The oldest institution for deaf people in the world. Supported in large measure by federal funds. A bastion of deaf culture and ASL. Has an extensive bookstore on deafness.

National Technical Institute for the Deaf (NTID)

Rochester Institute of Technology

One Lomb Memorial Drive

P.O. Box 9887

Rochester, NY 14623

Created by the Congress and funded by the U.S. Department of Education, it represents the first effort to educate deaf college students within a college campus designed primarily for hearing students. There are programs that are integrated with the Rochester Institute of Technology as well as self-contained classes for the deaf students.

Red Acre Farm Hearing Dog Center

P.O. Box 278

Stow, MA 01775

The center provides hearing ear dogs for the hearing impaired. These are dogs that are trained to respond to environmental noises, such as doorbells and alarms.

S. H. H. H. Self Help for Hard of Hearing People

7800 Wisconsin Avenue

Bethesda, MD 20814

A nonprofit organization that focuses on the needs of hard-of-hearing people, mainly adults. It provides a bimonthly publication. It is also concerned with education of the hearing public.

National Association of the Deaf

814 Thayer Avenue

Silver Spring, MD 20910

An association that supports programs for the deaf. Has a strong focus on total communication and ASL. Major concerns include legal and employment rights of deaf people.

Registry of Interpreters for the Deaf
51 Monroe Street, Suite 1107
Rockville, MD 20850
> Offers a national certification system for interpreters for deaf people. Maintains and distributes a registry of accredited interpreters.

National Cued Speech Association
P.O. Box 31345
Raleigh, NC 27622
> Provides information on cued speech and will help locate programs and teachers.

Deafness Research Foundation
9 E. 38th Street
New York, NY 10016
> Provides funds and support for research into the causes and cures of deafness.

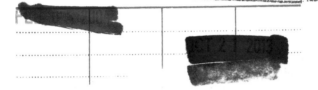